W9-AOM-929

Playback

PLAYBACK

Richard "Cactus" Pryor

University of Texas Press

AUSTIN

First edition, 1995

Requests for permission to reproduce material from this work
should be sent to Permissions, University of Texas Press, Box 7819,
Austin, TX 78713-7819.

∞ The paper used in this publication meets the minimum
requirements of American National Standard for Information
Sciences—Permanence of Paper for Printed Library Materials,
ANSI Z39.48-1984.

Library of Congress Cataloging-in-Publication Data

Pryor, Cactus
Playback / Richard "Cactus" Pryor. — 1st ed.
p.   cm.
Includes index.
ISBN 0-292-76567-3 (alk. paper)
I. Title.
PN1991.4.P68A25   1995
818'.5408—dc20   95-10561

Designed by Ellen McKie

In memory of my sister
MARY ALICE

Contents

Illustrations   ix

Foreword   xi

Acknowledgments   xiii

Introduction   1

1. A Half Century of Radio   3

2. A River Runs Through   8

3. The Family Secret   10

4. The Longest Laugh   13

5. Rubadubdub   17

6. The City of Angels   22

7. Seashells   25

8. Dangerously Live   27

9. Thanksgiving   31

10. Reunion on Maui   33

11. I Am You   40

12. Death in Louisville 43

13. Joshua's Shoes 47

14. The Net Caster 51

15. The Panhandle Pundit 54

16. Gift to George 60

17. Lufkin Man 63

18. There Is Hope 65

19. The Credit Card 70

20. The Naming 72

21. Fish Oil 75

22. Great Britain and Texas via Idaho 78

23. Déjà Vu 83

24. The 104-Year-Old Student 84

25. The Putting Preacher 87

26. Winter Beach 90

27. D-Day Fifty Years After 92

28. Eulogy to John 95

29. The Leper 100

30. Song-and-Dance Man 108

31. The Love Couple 112

32. The Duke of Wayne 114

33. Ambassador Davis 120

34. The Homeplace 124

35. A Conversation with Michener 129

36. The Visitors 136

37. Allison's Gift 139

38. Saltwater Mustangs 142

39. Washington, D.C., Taxi 145

40. The Loser 148

41. The Hands of Time 150

Index 155

Illustrations

Author at microphone, 1955 6
With Coach Darrell Royal 15
Walter Yates in Alaska 18
Donna Axum, Helen Hayes, and author 29
John Henry Faulk and friend 42
With Phyllis George 45
Interviewing Stanley Marsh 3 57
Aboard the *Sea? Si!* 76
David and Julia Hunter with Peggy and Cactus Pryor 81
The Reverend Dr. Gerald Mann 88
With John and Nellie Connally and newsman Frank Blair 96
"Skinny" Pryor, song-and-dance man 110
John "Duke" Wayne and "friendly Indians" 117
The Captain Billy Young House, Greenville, South Carolina 126
With Elizabeth Crook, James Michener, Liz Carpenter,
and Steve Harrigan 133
On Mustang Island 153

Foreword

here is a hike and bike trail along Town Lake on the Colorado River that flows through downtown Austin, Texas. Thousands of joggers, bicyclers, baby carriages, and dogs pass here daily, and some pause for a rest at the inviting bench set next to a clump of cactus plants.

Inscribed on a bronze plaque of rough-hewn granite are these words: "The Cactus Patch—in honor of Cactus Pryor, who brings laughter and good times to Texas." It was placed there by the Headliners Club, which honored its best-known master of ceremonies on its twenty-fifth anniversary. Lady Bird Johnson and I picked the bench instead of the past trite plaques and talked the Austin Parks and Recreation Department into this treasured spot. She had clout; I wrote the words.

Cactus Pryor has been our friend for more than half a century. Not only ours but a friend to people in cities and audiences all over Texas and miscellaneous places from the capital of politics in Washington, D.C., to the capital of show biz, Hollywood. His name, as well as his overflowing, finely chiseled wit, makes him unforgettable.

This book—*Playback*—has a wider appeal. Not only is it humor, it is life—peopled by the famous and obscure characters who surfaced for him in a lifetime of interviews and experiences. The reader meets James Michener in a ranch weekend with other authors. You know the Duke—John Wayne—who invited Cactus to be part of a movie with him. He introduces you to his preacher, his grandchildren, and a love couple he calls Mr. and Mrs. Schmertz, and all the while your own circle of friends grows.

You do all this in Cactus' vivid, clipped writing style where one word is used if that's all it takes. So it is easy and fast to read. But not so fast that you can miss the fact that this is a remarkable personality of insight, wit, and loyalty who has graced his country with a high heart and made it and its inhabitants better for it.

Acknowledgments

hen I consider those who have helped me with this book, I am inclined not to accept the title of author of *Playback*. I feel like a couple celebrating their fiftieth wedding anniversary. They want to invite to their party all those who have been an important part in their half-century marriage. However, they have room for only one hundred. Knowing it is incomplete, here is my party list of thank you's:

Marchese Guglielmo Marconi. Had he not invented the wireless I would not have written the essays nor conducted the interviews that appear in this book. Here's to you, Marky, whatever frequency you're now on.

Lady Bird Johnson, Luci Baines Johnson, Dave Morris, and Van Kennedy, who provided the microphones over the years and had the courage to allow me to use them without question. Well, almost without question.

All my crazy radio cohorts over the years who knew how to do a job and have fun at it, too.

All my crazy television cohorts over the years. Why didn't someone tell us we were pioneers? We would have been more dignified.

Bill Moyers, our cub reporter who through the years has encouraged me by example to be a better communicator. Why did you throw that firecracker under my chair when I was reading that newscast?

My brother Wally. He courageously directed me from the safe side of the cameras.

My dear, late friend John Henry Faulk. My mentor. And with his wonderful Lizzy always encouraging.

Steve Harrigan. He helped me get beyond the words and into feelings.

My kids: Paul, Kerry, Don, and Dayne. They shared their childhood . . . and many embarrassing family secrets . . . with my radio audience, which included their blushing mother, Jewell.

And the grandchildren, Allison, Ana Louise, Pecos, Elizabeth, and Marissa, who have inspired so many, many radio essays. Thanks Kerry, DorRhea, and Julie for having them.

Liz Carpenter. She taught me . . . JUST DO IT!

Darrell Royal, who gave me stories and reflected glory. Likewise the Duke.

Port Aransas and all its unshackled children who know how to enjoy life. And here's to the schools of king mackerel, redfish, and trout who annually give schools of Pryors great joy. My mother lode of essays.

Brother Arthur and sister Harriett, always reminding me not to take it too seriously.

James Michener, who actually labeled me an author!

Phyllis Dempsey, thanks for an index I could afford.

Joanna Hitchcock, the director of the University of Texas Press who had the courage to present this departure from "scholarly works" to a faculty committee and recommend it.

Speaking of the British, a toast with Scotch whiskey to the Hunters of London. A bonanza of adventures and stories.

My wife, Peggy, who rode the rough, the narrow, the slippery roads encountered in living so many of the stories and then in telling the stories. My co-pilot, my navigator, my friend, my critic, my prodder, my map folder, and my ever-persistent, and even sometimes successful, organizer.

And finally, a thank you to five generations of listeners. Keep them cards and letters comin' in, friends and neighbors out there in radio land.

Playback

Introduction

ompiling this book has not been easy. Many of the essays were not written; they were scribbled. Scribbled on airsickness bags, mostly unused, on paper napkins, and more than a few on toilet tissue. But in preparing this book, I dared to enter the world of high tech. I was an uneasy rider. I should have heeded the first sign. It came on Mustang Island off the Texas Coast. I had gone there for a week of isolation in order to begin all this. While unloading my laptop, I unloaded it on my toe top. My bare right big toe top. A black toe has been a constant reminder of my entry into the world of File, Edit, View, Insert, Format, Font, Tools, Window.

I am not high on high tech. I am a digital idiot adrift in a sea of technology that is carrying me to the edge of the world that Columbus was dumb enough to think didn't exist. I can't tell you the number of devastatingly clever and witty stories that I lost during this process, floating now like spoiled spume out there in the sea of lost stuff.

The great lesson I learned during my baptism into the church of Iconia is never to click your mouse on Help. You mouse that sucker, and you'll go down a yellow brick road of computerese gobbledygook that will confuse you to the point of Texas legislative mentality. Asking a computer for Help is like asking Saddam Hussein to come teach your Sunday school class. You, also, will never eat another apple in your life. Were it not for my computer guides, Willyn Wahl and Mike Dempsey, I would be sitting on top of a mountain muttering ahm mannie pahn ummms.

I tested the patience of my semisuffering wife, Peggy. She learned to interpret the problem by the intensity of my screams. "That's a 'the printer's not working' scream." "Oh, oh. That's a 'I've lost the whole damn thing' scream."

When her patience wore thin, I went to the old familiar refrain, "But this book was your idea."

For years I have delivered five commentaries a week on radio station KLBJ in Austin, Texas. Some of them are included here.

I have been a constant miner of people. As I traveled around the world to speak on banquet microphones, my battered tape recorder traveled with me. Like a poor man's Charles Kuralt, I mined the people I met. Interviews were done over the drone of airplane engines, in taxis, sometimes with the sound of water underneath or rushing by. I interviewed Liz Carpenter in a hot tub, and another subject in a bathtub (stay tuned for details). I have been privileged to meet and interview those who went for the brass ring and grabbed it. But more important, I captured on tape some of those more fortunate people who knew nothing of brass rings but had them in their grasp from the beginning.

I welcome this opportunity to share these words with you on these pages. Ear words now eye words.

ONE

A Half Century of Radio

ifty years ago, I began my career as a radio broadcaster, and I still marvel at the medium that has supported me. I still find it hard to believe that I can sit at a microphone and say words that will be heard by people hundreds of miles away, driving in automobiles, walking down country lanes, lying in bed, even swimming. A half century later, I find it remarkable that music can be transported through the air to be enjoyed by whoever chooses to hear it.

I have enjoyed my involvement in other media. I was a pioneer in television. I have been in a couple of John Wayne films, but it would be a stretch to label myself a cinematic actor. I am a writer. But radio is my baby. It's my favorite. It's intimate. It's just you and me, babe. Me in my house shoes and jeans talking to you in your bathrobe with your hair in curlers and mine in the top drawer of the dresser.

For years I broadcast a daily morning program from my home. My children, Paul, Kerry, Don, and Dayne, shared the microphone with me in that order, beginning with goo-goo's and graduating to boo-boo's. My late wife, Jewell, was in a constant state of anxiety, wondering what family secret would next be shared with the whole community. "Daddy, why did Uncle Bert sleep on the front porch last night?"

I took my microphone down to the streets for Man on the Street interviews. Curb service talk radio . . . and Rush Limbaugh wasn't even born. I dodged chairs and mattresses being thrown from hotel windows overhead as we celebrated the end of World War II, and I interviewed proud American victors.

I still shudder when I recall one broadcast from the main street of Alice, Texas. I asked a woman what she thought of our sponsor, the Queen Alice Coffee Shop. She told me in words that melted the chrome on the microphone. Had I only known that she had just been fired as a waitress there. Early radio four-letter words.

Alice wasn't easy. The Hispanic host of our Spanish-language program prospered amazingly for one of such small salary. We accidentally discovered the reason when we learned he was getting money for requests and announcements: five dollars for weddings, ten dollars for funerals. So we halved it with him.

My news editor, Mike Holberg, and I, just back from the war, found a new one in that South Texas town. We exposed a deputy sheriff for his gambling indiscretions. He gave us "till sundown to get out of town." We did. My successor didn't. He was killed by that deputy sheriff on the main street of Alice. There's virtue in cowardice.

Border radio and television in the Lower Rio Grande Valley brought us unique management problems caused by the proximity to Mexico with all its temptations. A disc jockey tried to smuggle a lady of the evening from one nation to another in the trunk of his car. "Oh, her! I'd forgotten that she came over with me." And there was our copywriter who experienced incredible bust development in a few hours across the Rio Grande. The border patrol found her stash of marijuana when an agent noted that she was better endowed returning from than going to Mexico.

I remember introducing General Douglas McArthur on network radio from the steps of the Texas state capitol. I was so nervous, I screwed it up. "Ladies and gentlemen, I present to you General Arthur McDouglas." I was never meant for the military.

I will forever recall the day our microphones described the bloody hours when the Tower of the Main Building of the University of Texas became the fort for a deranged sniper. Our news editor, Paul Bolton, when giving the names of the fatalities, read the name of his own grandson and stayed on the job.

We introduced the first black disc jockey to Houston radio on KNUZ. Police escorted him home. Crosses were burned and threats were rampant. A barrier came down, and a vast untapped market was opened, and every weak-minded bigot in Houston spewed venom.

On the sad day of the assassination of John Kennedy, I broadcast the scene from the LBJ Ranch on the Pedernales River, where I was to have emceed a program of entertainment at a barbecue in his honor the next day. That ranch suddenly became the home of the new president of the United States.

I remember reporting the death of the husband of the owner of the radio station where I've spent most of these fifty years, Lady Bird Johnson. And then a few days later, I served as a people spotter for Charles Kuralt, who covered the funeral for CBS.

Those were heady moments when I was occasionally invited to guest on Arthur Godfrey's show on the entire CBS network. High cotton. He was unknowingly my radio mentor, he the master of the soft pitch. His pitches to his crew during the breaks—not so soft.

But it's the bizarre moments I remember most vividly. The interview with Jane Fonda in Austin. It was during the Vietnamese War. She was as popular as a live grenade. I had scheduled her for a thirty-minute live radio appearance. She arrived at the station wearing a mega mad. She had just participated in

Author at microphone, 1955.

a television interview with my friend the Reverend Dr. Gerald Mann. He had challenged her challenging our involvement in Vietnam. And now here she was at the radio station of the wife of the man who was commander in chief of our armed services, to be interviewed by some redneck with the bucolic name of Cactus. I greeted her with, "I've been looking forward to our interview, Miss Fonda."

She mortally wounded my enthusiasm with eye darts as she spewed, "You have five minutes."

"But we had arranged for a thirty-minute interview."

"You have five minutes."

We sat at the microphone. The on-the-air sign came on. I said, "Before we get to the interview, Miss Fonda, I would like to say something to you."

"What?" she spat.

"I would like to say that I admire you. I admire your courage in stating your convictions. I may or may not agree with them, but in the face of all the criticism and threats that you have received for exercising free speech, I consider you a courageous and concerned American."

Her fists became hands, and her hunched shoulders relaxed, and a smile appeared on her intense face. Thirty minutes later, we concluded the interview.

Then there was the thirty-minute interview that I changed to a two-minute interview. It was with actor Dan Dailey. He was performing at a local dinner theater. He arrived for a 9:00 A.M. interview looking as happy as a vegetarian at a barbecue. As we came on the air, I said, "Welcome, Dan. Do you enjoy doing dinner theater?"

That inspired, "No."

"Uh, well is it because you don't like the hours involved, like getting up early to be on radio shows? Ha, ha, ha."

"Yes."

"Well, uh . . . tell me, Mr. Dailey, was it easier making movies than doing theater?"

"No."

A couple more minutes of nothing but yes or no responses. I said, "Mr. Dailey, you don't really want to be here, do you?"

He replied, "No."

"Well, actually I'm not enjoying you either. So let's conclude the interview."

We did. I enjoyed doing that.

It's a strange way to make a living, sitting at a desk while talking into a metal object. Never seeing those who are listening to you . . . or even knowing that they are listening. Sometimes you are talking only to yourself, but it's okay for others to listen. And in between, trying to cram a ninety-second commercial into sixty seconds.

I began broadcasting in 1944. My employer . . . still my employer, still my friend . . . Lady Bird Johnson. A great lady. My life's work identifiable by alphabetical letters . . . KNOW, KTBC, KBKI, KSIX, KNUZ, KLBJ, KTBC-TV, KVUE-TV. Now, please stay tuned for the fifty-first year, friends and neighbors out there in radio land.

TWO

A River Runs Through

river flows through my office window. It runs continuously in two directions . . . north and south. I can hear the rumble of its rushing current through the double panes, but only faintly. If I could open my windows, the noise would be intolerable.

It's a busy river: crafts carrying their cargoes to all points north, south, east, and west. At night it is a necklace of lights . . . twin strands reflecting off the glass panes. It hasn't got a romantic name like Shenandoah, Swanee, Jordan. Its name is numerical: IH 35.

Often, when I am a part of this cement river, I curse it as it sweeps me along through whirlpools and tidal waves and tries to add me to its flotsam and jetsam. But I am fascinated by the sight of it. An incredible number of eighteen-wheelers pass through our city . . . a lamentable fact. The most evident, the big Wal-Mart trucks heading to or from their huge center a few miles south . . . the mother lode feeding the Wal-Mart stores of the nation. Mom and pop be damned!

I watch the never-ceasing flow. Mobile billboards, the eighteen-wheelers. A montage of commercials. That one shouts Longhorn Disposal . . . then Federal Express . . . Haliburton . . . J. C. Penney . . . CFI. A renter drives a billboard, Hertz, . . . then Mayflower, Central, Allied, and here comes Mr. Move It. Then Pearl Beer, H.E.B., Frito-Lay, Armour, Fish . . . a movable feast.

Now a rescuer carries a wounded dump truck on its back . . . an eight-wheel litter.

Japan passes every few seconds . . . Toyota, Mazda, Mitsubishi, Nissan, Suzuki. The United Nations of automobiles in review: Mercedes, Volvo, Volkswagen, Ferrari, Porsche, Lexus. And let's hear it for America! Chevrolet, Ford, Pontiac, Dodge, Chrysler, Buick, Lincoln, Plymouth, Cadillac. A jungle of Jaguars and Cougars. A herd of Pintos and Mustangs.

And there goes a brave or foolish man on a motorbike . . . a gnat in an elephant stampede.

There goes a dinosaur carrying twelve baby dinosaurs piggyback.

Now, outside my window, a motorcyclist lies in the lurch . . . an electronic gun aimed at the river. He's spotted his target and off he goes, red light flashing. His hunt will be successful.

The river flashes red too often. The roar is drowned by the wail of a siren. A victim of the river . . . a rescue.

Just now, another human drama. A battered veteran of the mechanical wars . . . a family heading south from a north that has betrayed them. Its space filled with children. On top a mattress tied with a rope, and it pulls a makeshift trailer filled with their belongings. Grapes of Wrath 1994.

There walks a would-be passenger, his belongings in a knapsack, his thumb extends toward the road but his face looks ahead. They don't know how to hitchhike nowadays.

On and on flows the cement river, its hunger fed by ports throughout our land.

Is that the sound of cattle? Yes, a cattle truck loaded with South Texas beef heading up the paved river that was once the Chisholm Trail . . . Is that Little Joe the Wrangler at the wheel?

THREE

The Family Secret

ntil it became part of my job description, I avoided cemeteries. I had always believed that visiting them was something you should put off as long as possible. However, when but a youthful bass, I auditioned and earned a job singing with a funeral-home quartet. It usually was an easy gig. You stood behind a curtain, often in tennis shoes and shorts, and sang the traditional songs that accompanied the deceased from here to whichever direction he was going. We came with the casket, the limousine, and the flowers. Occasionally, however, we were required to accompany the funeral party to the cemetery and sing until the final curtain had lowered. Once I had arrived ready for a game of tennis following the service only to learn that we were to perform at the cemetery. I was not dressed for the occasion. But I soon was when the funeral director outfitted me in one of the many suits available for the stars of coming attractions. I thought, "My gawd! I'm a test pilot for a dead man."

When I learned that my new wife, Peggy, loved visiting cemeteries, I had my first serious apprehensions about our relationship. However, we returned one Memorial Day to the small country cemetery cut out of the pines of southern Arkansas where we had buried her father a few months before. It is a peaceful place. On that holiday, there is always an endless medley of familiar old hymns floating across the road from a small country church, a serenade to the families who have come to visit their departed. Fresh flowers are placed upon the graves, replacing the faded plastic ones. Reunions with old friends are held. Some folks bring picnic lunches. It is not a sad scene. It is a comforting visit . . . a reunion. So when Peggy, on a beautiful spring day, suggested that we take my mother and visit my father's grave, I was happy to go.

We had no directions . . . only my mother's recollections, and they were faded. However in searching for the Pryors, we discovered mother's family, the Christoffersens. There underneath a small tree was the tombstone of the lady who was born in Denmark in 1861 and who died in Austin, Texas, in 1962. At first glance, the viewer's impression is, "Poor child. She lived only one year." But then the dates soak in: 101 years . . . and Ana Christina Christoffersen made most of them prime years . . . even when they weren't. Next to her, Grandpa Thomas Christoffersen. He wasn't really my grandfather because grandmother outlived three husbands. On the other side of Ana's grave, Uncle Albert. He had had eighty-five years. And next to him, a weathered tombstone: Grandma's other son. He lived but twenty-two years. The gold star always in Grandma's window read as the tombstone: Sergeant Marinus Thompson . . . killed in Argonne Forest, France, 1918.

Our reverie was interrupted by Peggy's voice. She had located the Pryor plot. We hurried over. And there she was . . . the consummate matriarch . . . Grandma Pryor. Caroline Wallace Pryor. Born Greenville, South Carolina, before the Civil War and left Carolina because of it. Surrounding her grave are the tombstones of her sisters, Fanny, Alethea, Josephine. And there, the graves of Aunt Roberta and Aunt Maude (she told us she was dying for over fifty years) . . . she made it to eighty-five. And Aunt Florence and Aunt Julia. And there the tombstone of my dad. "Here lies Richard "Skinny" Pryor. Masterful Showman." And that he was, this old song-and-dance man. Next to him, his brother Wallace . . . born two years to the day later than Dad. And died two years earlier to the day of Dad's death.

As I gazed upon these markers of my family's graves, I thought how proud they were of their Southern heritage. They were of the Confederacy and never forgot it. I never understood that pride nor why they would refer to those who freed the slaves as "damn Yankees and poor white trash." For what reasons did my family have this attitude of Southern aristocracy? I thought aristocrats came with wealth.

Amid the familial forest of tombstones an ancient one, small . . . leaning precariously toward Aunt Roberta (and the closer to Roberta you got, the more precarious it was). We couldn't read the inscription, so Peggy took a piece of paper and a pencil and did a rubbing. And lo, the family secret came forth: "John Pryor, Corporal, Company A, 17TH Illinois Cavalry." My God! Grandfather was a Union soldier! That's why the family never talked about my grandfather. Grandmother had married a Yankee soldier! And all through my life, they had tried to protect me from this scandalous reality.

I was filled with a warm glow of belated pride. Grandfather had fought against slavery. I've got Yankee blood in my veins!

As we were leaving, I just had to whistle a chorus of "Yankee Doodle." This one's for you, Grandpa John.

FOUR

The Longest Laugh

s an interviewer, I hate the "What was" question. "What was your most embarrassing . . . what was your most memorable . . . what was your most valuable . . ." They should be responded to with, "What was the most stupid question you ever asked other than the one you just asked?"

Having so stated, let me tell you what was the longest laugh I ever heard. It came as a response to one who is not in the business of making laughs, though he can be awfully effective in producing them. He is Darrell Royal, legendary former football coach at the University of Texas, with whom I had the pleasure of co-hosting his weekly television show for a number of years. DKR, as he is initially known, is noted for his down-home humor and sayings. As a matter of fact, his "dance with the one what brung you" saying (don't change offenses in the middle of a season) became the title of a book.

Darrell inherited his vast repertoire of folksy sayings in his grandmother's house in Oklahoma where he was reared. He says it was the way everyone talked back home. Certainly his grand-mother talked the talk of the people of the Dust Bowl country. It's the language of those who knew the value of laughter to survival.

A sense of humor serves you well in the game of football, too. My diminutive friend Jaston Williams of *Greater Tuna* fame attests to that. When asked how he acquired his sense of humor, he explained, "When you grow up in West Texas and are too small to play football, you better have a sense of humor."

The press loved DKR for his colorful phrases. After a loss, "Our whoa was all right, but we didn't have any go." Sayings like, "He's making enough money to burn a wet elephant." "He's big enough to burn diesel." "He doesn't have a whole lot of speed, but maybe Elizabeth Taylor can't sing." "You spend your time waiting for these promising players to deliver, and pretty soon you're wearing a straw hat to Christmas."

Darrell Royal was dead serious about winning football games, and he won more than any coach in the rich history of the University of Texas. But when he lost, he always had a way of expressing his feelings—on his television show or at the weekly Longhorn Club meetings after the games--with humor. Following one loss, he told the alumni assembled, "Glad to see you orange bloods here . . . and next of kin. I know some of you probably came just to see what the son-of-a-bitch would say today."

But on to the longest laugh. Texas had lost to two of their most bitter rivals in 1971. In answering a question regarding the losses at a meeting of the Longhorn Club, Darrell had them rolling in the aisles. Each year the Headliners Club of Austin had its annual luncheon. The newsmakers and news coverers of the state joined with national personalities such as Walter Cronkite, John Wayne, Lucille Ball, or Gregory Peck for roast and ribbing. I asked Royal if he would reproduce on film the remark he had made at the Longhorn Club. He consented.

I informed the audience assembled for the Headliners lun-cheon that Coach Royal had filmed a statement for television

With Coach Darrell Royal. Photo by James Koch.

regarding recent losses. Because of its importance, I knew they'd want us to share the film with them. In making the film, we had used the same setting that he used every week following the game to answer questions from reporters.

The question was posed by an off-camera reporter, "Coach, after losing to both your alma mater Oklahoma and to Arkansas, how do you feel?"

The camera came in for a close-up of the incredibly sincere face of Coach Royal. It showed the great pain of defeat. His voice was subdued and measured. The Headliners audience watching the film was caught up in the drama of what they were seeing. They were surprised to be witnessing such a sober episode at the usually hilarious luncheon.

Royal said, "Of course, these two losses that have been dealt to us, first by Oklahoma, and then by Arkansas, which was a lopsided defeat, caused us to do a lot of reflecting and a lot of thinking. I was reading a story that a young man was interviewing Oliver Wendell Holmes, and Oliver Wendell Holmes told this young man that if he had a method, a surefire method, by which he could cause the world to bypass all troubles, that he wouldn't pass this formula on to the public or even to his friends because he felt that everyone needed some trouble in their life. And, you know, this story causes you to do some serious thinking, and I have, and my thought is: piss on Oliver Wendell Holmes."

First, there was a vacuum of silence, followed by a collective gurgle. And then, an explosion of laughter that grew and grew and exploded again. I waited for the incredible roar to subside for five full minutes. Royal had caught them with their defense down and had scored a Super Bowl touchdown. Anyone on the program after that was doomed. It was the longest laugh I've ever heard.

FIVE

Rubadubdub

've done strange interviews for radio and television. There was the one with columnist Heloise, in her apartment in Washington, in her closet, under a blanket. Not what you might think. We were merely trying to shut out the noise of the planes landing at nearby National Airport. A TV pardner, Barbara Miller, and I interviewed Liz Carpenter in her Jacuzzi, she and Barbara in their bathing suits, me in coat and tie.

But I went all the way to Alaska to grab this one. It was with my friend Walter Yates. He had gone to Alaska to break away . . . from the pain of a marriage gone sour; from the boredom of covering floors with carpeting; from the suffocation of daily rituals that were contrary to the rhythms of a pilot, fisherman, hunter, and adventurer. "So enough. I'm outta here. I'm off to Alaska. With the same tools with which my grandfather built his cabin in the Ozarks of Arkansas, I will build my own cabin. I will get as far away from civilization as I can. I will spend the entire

Walter Yates in Alaska. Courtesy Walter Yates.

Arctic winter in isolation. I will trap. I will explore. I will, hopefully, find the serenity that has eluded me now too damn long." So he did.

We were neighbors and friends. Our children played together. We had adventures together. Taking off from a sandy wheel-grabbing beach adjacent to the King Ranch after a fishing trip, only a heaven-sent gust of air kept us from hitting another plane parked at the end of our takeoff stretch. Once we inadvertently flew through a front that contained numerous tornadoes that destroyed scores of planes on the ground. We still don't know what kept us from joining the number. So when Walter decided to embark on this adventure, I wanted to at least have a small hand in it.

Walter planned to make a movie of his winter in the wilderness. He rigged his camera so that he could film himself by remote control. However, a small production crew flew to Alaska to film the beginning of his months of aloneness. I interviewed him on camera as we sat around a campfire in front of his cabin on the Post River, two hundred miles northwest of Anchorage.

The game plan called for a friend of Walter's in Anchorage to fly him to his cabin, drop him off, and pick him up, hopefully, after the next thaw.

I also recorded a radio interview with Walter to paint a word picture of the site that would be his home for the long winter months. It went like this:

"Walter, as we sit here by the campfire watching Silver Creek bubbling along just below your cabin . . . and see the marble-sized blueberries all around us . . . and feel the warmth of the sun, have you considered that winter will change all this?"

"Yes, Cactus, I have. I know this happy little creek that we're listening to right now will become silent. I know that the blueberries will soon be gone. Likewise, the sun. I know that I will live mostly in a frozen darkness. I know that my life will depend on, among other things, that huge cache of wood I have cut over there. Matter of fact, it's getting kinda chilly now. Let me put another log on the fire. And I know that the roar of Post River down there in the valley . . . I think your microphone can pick up the sound . . . I know that, too, will become part of the silence. I realize that a lot of animals I'm seeing daily will be hibernating. Look up there on the side of that mountain, Cactus. That one right over there. Can you see those sheep?"

"Where, Walter?"

"Look up to the very top of that mountain there. Now come down to about three o'clock. See those little white dots?"

"Oh, yeah. I see them now."

"Well, those are the famous Dall sheep of Alaska. I don't imagine I'll be seeing them during the winter. Look at 'em frolicking, would you?"

"Yeah. It's like gravity is not a factor with them. As white as they are, you wouldn't be able to see them against the snow, even if they stick around."

"Pass the coffee pot over here, so I can pour another cup, will you? Careful now. Don't burn your fingers. Can I pour you a cup? Here you are. Tastes better in a tin cup, doesn't it? Anyway, I know I will be living in a different world than the one we're in right now. Look at the sun just beginning to hunker down behind Peaceful Mountain over there. In a few weeks, it'll slip down behind it, and I won't see it again till spring. I look around me, and I soak in the beauty of those birch trees across the river there with their golden leaves. Look at that blue sky and those puffy white clouds. And the reflection of the sun bouncing off of Silver Creek. Well, I'm soaking all of this beauty in, so I can remember it when my world becomes all white. And . . . hold on. Look what's coming down the trail on the other side of the river."

"Where, Walter? I don't see anything."

"Look right over there by that big rock."

"Oh, yeah. It's a caribou!"

"Right. And notice how his head is drooping. He's been cut out of the herd, and he's on the lam. Now let's watch, and you'll see what's going on."

"Man, he looks tuckered out. Like he's been running for a long time."

"He has. And look there. That's why he's running. See it?"

"What is it, a dog?"

"No, that's a wolf. He's a big one. Notice he's not running very fast. Just a steady lope. That caribou will be supper tonight. Look how graceful he is."

"Hey, you! Get the hell outta here. This is private territory."

"Save your breath, Cactus. He's on a hot trail. Besides, he can't hear you for the rushing water."

"Another example of the survival of the fittest. Well, Walter, the sun has set. I can already feel the cold seeping in, and the fire has just about died out. And . . . hey, look. The moon's coming a'calling."

"Yep. Maybe that's a good omen. Thanks for coming to say adios for awhile."

"Good luck to you, old friend. I'll be thinking about you all winter long."

And that's the interview my radio audience heard. It was a sham. It was not recorded on the Post River. It was recorded in a bathtub. When we were at his cabin, I discovered that I had left my recorder in my hotel room in Anchorage. So, not to waste the opportunity, Walter and I decided to create the interview from Post River in Anchorage. After testing, we discovered that the only place we could achieve the proper outdoor sound was in the bathtub with the shower curtain drawn. So while sitting there, fully dressed, we saw the blueberries, the colored leaves, the rushing waters. We saw the caribou and the wolf . . . the Dall sheep . . . the setting sun and the rising moon. Only the time and the site were wrong. The interview was past tense for we had seen all those sights we described while two hundred miles northwest of the bathtub in which we now sat. Back in the studio in Texas, I added the sounds of rushing water, campfire crackling, breezes, and coffee pouring. We considered it a technological white lie.

Truthfully, Walter Yates survived the winter and came out of the wilderness a man at peace with the world. His video *Breakaway* is now available. Incidentally, we have not since shared a bathtub with each other.

SIX

The City of Angels

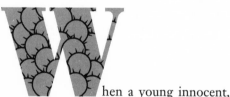hen a young innocent,
I went to UCLA to learn radio and how not to talk like a Texan.
In 1945 Los Angeles was a wild and crazy town. Why it was
nothing at all to see at least three or four guys a day wearing a
long beard and sandals. You could see women smoking little
black cigars. White guys with black women and white women
with black guys. We even saw one woman hitchhiking! I wrote
home about this one: "We went to dinner and some woman,
probably a movie star, came in wearing shorts and high heels.
You could almost see the outline of her nipples under her tight
blouse." I wrote that one to my brothers, of course.

"And get this, brother. One of the girls in my announcing
class asked one of the guys for a date! Wild, eh?"

I went back to Los Angeles recently. At least, that's how the
pilot identified it. You couldn't see it for the smog. Didn't much
look like L.A. on the ground, either. I remember that you could
see the mountains from downtown Sunset Boulevard back in 1945.

The mountains had disappeared. Westwood Village, where I had lived and gone to classes, was gone, too. Somebody moved a bunch of skyscrapers where there used to be trees and houses like grandmother's. And the orange trees. I can remember an almost continuous grove of orange trees from L.A. to San Diego. The only oranges I could find all these years later were in a supermarket . . . and they were from the Lower Rio Grande Valley in Texas.

After twenty-four hours of amazed return, I concluded that the Los Angeles city limits sign should include an addendum. It should read: This City Is Rated R.

L.A. is one big perfume or aftershave TV commercial. Long-legged women in tight jeans and high heels are as numerous as Toyotas on the freeways. Miniskirts are back in—and up—in L.A. There's a whole new dimension to girl-watching . . . they offer so much more to watch. Everywhere you go, there are bulging muscles and flared nostrils. And likewise, the guys.

Cars are sexy. Convertibles come complete with blonde flying hair. I actually met a person who had natural-colored hair. He was a bellboy at the Beverly Hilton who had arrived only the week before from Tibet.

Wrinkles are apparently not allowed. If all the facelifts in L.A. collapsed at the same time, California would hurtle into the sea halfway to Hawaii.

Billboards look like the centerfold of *Playboy* . . . or *girl*. One television anchorwoman could have reported the imminent end of the world, and I would not have gotten the message. Her looks made the stories incidental.

I saw a policewoman who made you rack your brain for some minor crime you could commit right then and there. Apprehend me . . . search me, please!

Mannequins in store windows would make Hugh Heffner blush.

Language is sexy. "Rooms Available with a View of Whomever." "Video Date Clubs . . . Taped Dates." "Church Services for Singles Only." "Amazing Grace, Incredible Helen." "Body Painting . . . Yours or Ours."

And, of course, the beach scene. Hormones run amok. Bare-bottomed bikinis, the latest muscles, and G-strings for the guys . . . and that's ten miles before you reach the beach. Humanity passes on roller blades.

You name it; L.A. presents it. A smorgasbord of everything you won't find at home. Herds and herds of the typical girl next door . . . if you live next door to Sharon Stone.

In the land where Dorothy and I went down the yellow brick road in 1945, there are some new, weird characters. The tin man is now the Teflon man with gold chains. The straw man is down to his last few straws and flaunting it. The cowardly lion is now a wolf, sometimes in Dorothy's clothing. And Dorothy? Well, Dorothy should catch the next tornado and go back to the farm in Kansas.

SEVEN

Seashells

hat this world needs is more seashells. What is it about wading in the beach shallows, peering downward, hoping to spot that certain seashell you want, or anticipating a wonderful serendipity? Why is this pastime so intriguing . . . so healing . . . so universal?

Seashells bring people together like a magical magnet. Collectors, like the shells they seek, come in all shapes and sizes and ages. Mothers walking hand in hand with their daughters. Fathers wrapping weathered hands around the tender hands of their sons. Older couples still holding dearly to one another, picking up the pieces left by the sea.

A big hulk of a man, beer belly hanging over his bucking bronco belt buckle; stub of a cigar in his mouth; polyester pants rolled up to his knobby knees; groaning as he bends over to tenderly pick up a delicate shell and breaking into a broad grin as he holds it up to be appreciated.

Tiny tots with their buckets. They don't have to be taught.

It comes with the genes . . . it comes with the species. Seashells are for collecting. It seems that each year we produce a new collector. Seashell collectors: Paul, Kerry, Don, Dayne, Julie, Stuart, Julie II, Allison, Ana Louise, Pecos, Elizabeth, Marissa, and my shell protégé, my wife, Peggy, from Arkansas, where they have very few seashells.

The serious collectors. The frequent gatherers who know to dig down underneath the sand for that special shell . . . know the seasons in which to find them . . . know to examine the seaweed for others.

You can easily spot the newcomers. A half of a sand dollar will do. Fifty cents is enough.

My son Dayne, when young, would erect each summer a stand made out of driftwood and sell broken shells at a bargain rate. Logical. On the fifth of July, he sold used fireworks.

I am a toe pusher. I seldom collect shells. We have enough of them in the family to cover a virgin beach. But I do look for them as I stroll the coastal sands . . . and rather than bend down to pick one up I am content to nudge them with my toe, as lovingly as a toe nudge can be. I just want to see what's on the other side.

Seashells inspire poems, music. Inspired Anne Morrow Lindbergh to write her beautiful book, *Gifts from the Sea.* Inspire artisans to arrange them in fanciful form. But when the youngsters come in, their dripping buckets full of their treasures from the sandy beaches, the romance can soon retreat. For seashells, despite their beauty, most often come with little critters inside . . . little critters that don't adapt to a dry environment . . . and their *unadaptability* soon becomes evident by a less-than-endearing fragrance. And the youngsters howl in anguish when you return the seashells to the seashore.

Why the allure of finding seashells? Perhaps it's a primal instinct, pulling us back to where we began. Darwin would say that it's a reunion . . . a family reunion. Maybe that's it . . . we're collecting kinfolk.

Dangerously Live

ive television is dangerous. In the days before video tape, every moment that you were on camera was fraught with potential disaster. In the early 1950s, we were living such hazardous lives. Consider: I was doing a thirty-minute live variety show every evening in prime time, locally. Even local has prime time. I had a five-piece band, singers, dancers, guests, commercials, and two cameras. All this live without rehearsal. The fact that my director, my brother Wally, and I remained friends is a miracle of familial compatibility. The studio was hardly larger than a psychiatrist's waiting room. We could hardly accommodate the sideburns of Elvis Presley and his band of leather-clad musicians when they made an appearance on my show. I knew the guy would never make it.

You were always haunted by the knowledge that if you fouled up you shared it with the entire community. And, oh, how we accommodated them. Former Miss America Donna Axum co-hosted a daily show with me, *High Noon II*. (Later Carolyn Jackson and I did *High Noon Rides Again*, and Barbara Miller and I broadcast *Son of High Noon*.) On one occasion, two of Donna's and my guests were to be folksingers Shane and Kitty. Kitty arrived on time, but Shane didn't. It was show time, and Shane was no show. So I said to Donna, on camera, "I'll be Shane. Introduce us." Donna was a preparer. That's one of the codes of Miss Americanism: be prepared. She was still smarting from the boo-boo she had committed on the last show, when we were told that we had time for one more number from our guest, who was a blind piano player. Donna asked him if he knew "Three Blind Mice." But there was no time for preparation. I took my stance beside Kitty. The camera came in for a close-up of Donna's beautiful face as she said, "And now, we are proud to present that wonderful folk team of Kane and Shitty."

Had it been the era of color television, the audience would have noticed that beautiful face turning orange, then red, and then a sort of algae green. I said, "You wanna try that again, Donna?" Donna did not want to try it again.

She got her revenge. She booked a snake. A huge boa constrictor snake. She knew I have had a snake phobia ever since that other television snake experience. So in the interview with the snake handler, I participated from the other side of the studio.

The other snake experience? It wasn't my show. It was Uncle Jay's show. Uncle Jay filled the studio with children every afternoon. Weekly he had the owner of a local zoo bring in critters to show the kids. This day the zookeeper brought in a glass aquarium full of snakes. Incidentally, Uncle Jay did not do his show that day. Our sports editor, Dan Love, filled in for him. Uncle Jay didn't like snakes anymore than he liked kids. Our aquarium-like viewing room above the studio was filled with mothers of the children below. And what those mothers saw . . . as well as the television audience . . . was the zoo man stumble on a television cable and drop the aquarium, thus releasing scores of "poisonous" snakes to attack their children. They also saw the snake man valiantly trying to recapture the snakes, which

Donna Axum, Helen Hayes, and author. Photo by Frank Armstrong.

were biting his hands, from which blood was streaming. Actually, the snakes were nonpoisonous, and the blood was from glass cuts. Dan Love and his partner, Packer Jack, developed on-site, instantaneous cases of snake phobia. They vacated the studio and were last seen trying to take the first bus out of town from the bus station across the street. I was paged to report to the studio immediately. As I entered, I could hear the deafening screams of the frantic mothers overhead. I saw a floor squirming with live snakes. I was handed a carton of Superior Dairies milk and was instructed to ad-lib a commercial. Both I and the milk clabbered. I have had a milk allergy ever since. Dan Love did not substitute for Uncle Jay again . . . ever.

Then there was the Smucker's jelly commercial. "Smucker's" is a scary word to say on the air. My co-hostess for *High Noon I* was Jean Boone. Jean didn't laugh, she snorted. As we began our two-person pitch for Smucker's jelly, we thought of the potential danger of the name. And we got tickled. I don't mean kinda tickled. I mean down on your knees, holding your sides, pants-wetting, pure-dee tickled. A tickled Boone is a series of snorts that would stampede a herd of horses. My laugh is a falsetto. I laugh like most rock singers sing. And there we stood for five torturous minutes as my cruel brother Wally kept the cameras locked on us. Jean snorting and me high C'ing. The entire audience of Central Texas' only television station was locked in one big Richter Scale–moving guffaw. There was no place to hide. The sale of Smucker's jelly skyrocketed in our town.

Every Saturday morning, anyone with talent to share was invited in for an audition. We felt an obligation to showcase local talent, for both the performer and the audience.

We hired untested people and allowed them to earn as they learned. One was a youngster from East Texas named Bill Moyers. We gave him a Polaroid camera and a pair of roller skates. He was our mobile news unit, and he covered Central Texas like cedar pollen. We urged a young announcer named Vern Lundquist to try his hand at sports announcing.

When a deranged killer with a small arsenal started shooting people from the top of the University of Texas Tower, our reporters not only reported the story they helped pull the wounded from the line of fire.

Our news editor, Paul Bolton, while reading the list of fatalities, read the name of his own grandson. He remained on the job.

We did many things simply because we didn't know we couldn't do them. We were unaware that we were pioneers crossing the deserts of a whole new frontier that was changing the United States forever. All we knew was that it was a helluva lot of fun. Imagine, people in your own hometown asking you for your autograph! The tube had arrived.

NINE

Thanksgiving

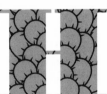

ow was your Thanksgiving? Ours was a little complicated. You see, we did the traditional. We went over the river and through the wood to grandfather's house. But we made the mistake of assuming that the horse knew the way. Now he did know the way, but it was the route to grandfather's old house, the one he and grandmother had when they were still married to each other. Grandmother now lives in the Bahamas with an Arthur Murray dance instructor. She moved after the old family place produced a horizontal hole gusher. Grandpa had left her to marry the widow who lived near the wood. Grandpa moved in with her . . . and the horse took us to the old place.

Well, little Ann and John are living there now. Little John just lost his job at the savings and loan, so he had to move into the old family place. And Ann had a fight with her live-in boyfriend (she was living in his pad). . . so she moved back to the old family home, also.

Some things remain. Ol' Jawler heard the bells of our sleigh and came running to meet us. Ol' Jawler got the family into hot water. He bit Ann's former live-in when he came to get the car that Ann claimed was half hers. Now he's suing the family for allowing a dangerous dog to run free, and Ann is suing him for her half of the car.

Anyway, Ann and John joined us, and we finally found grandfather's new living place. His new bride wasn't there because she was spending Thanksgiving with her daughter who lives in L.A. . . . her husband had just left her. And the maid who was going to cook Thanksgiving dinner for grandfather didn't show up. Her ex-husband who was her husband before this ex-husband found her at the house of the ex-husband who was her husband before this ex-husband was . . . and there was a big fight, and they were all down at municipal court taking out peace bonds against one another.

Sister was late for dinner because her ex-husband had the morning period to be with their daughter. He was two hours late bringing her back. But she finally arrived, her toes and nose stinging from the cold wind, since the power lift windows on the car weren't working.

We did have a turkey. Got it smoked and ready to eat at the delicatessen. We didn't have the pudding and pumpkin pie. Grandpa's cholesterol and triglyceride count is high since he started drinking again. So we had to watch that.

But we made do. We kissed them all, and we played snowball. I guess you could say we had, if not a first-rate, a second-rate play. And we did all sing "Hurrah for Thanksgiving Day," but it was a little off-key.

TEN

Reunion on Maui

t was easier for Lindbergh
to find Paris in the *Spirit of St. Louis* than it was for us to find his
burial place on the island of Maui. The simplified road map that
the rental car agent had given me indicated that it was just a
short junket from the Maui airport to the village of Hana on the
windward side of the island. I had been told that the grave of
Charles Lindbergh was not very far past Hana. What the map
did not tell me was that Charles Lindbergh's most courageous
trip was not flying the Atlantic. It was driving that road overlooking the Pacific that leads to his home on Maui.

The day my late wife, Jewell, and I drove it the Hana High-
way was worse than usual. There had been heavy rains that day
in the rain forests that the road skirts on its winding way, and
flooding had caused road damage. More rain was expected. We
did not know this. We were to become imminently aware of
that fact.

There are six hundred potential heart attack turns and fifty-six one-way bridges in the sixty-five miles from Paia on the northern coast to Hana. We were to learn that it is even further to the settlement of Kipahula, where Lindbergh lived. I've known people broader than that road. There is a saying in the islands, "Kipahula is far from Waikiki" . . . a world-class understatement.

The view along the way was magnificent. I know because Jewell told me so. My eyes were glued to the road crisis of the moment. There were many such moments. At several points, we had to wait long periods of time for workers to clear huge boulders from the road. Other times we had to stop and wait for just-born waterfalls that came gushing down the roadway to run themselves out before we could continue on. There was no way we could turn around. There was no around. Only forward or down . . . way down.

We did come to one turnout. We were surprised to see a car parked there. As we pulled into the small area, the driver opened the door and approached. She was crying desperately. "Please, sir, can you help me? I simply can't drive any further. I am frightened to death. I was going to photograph Lindbergh's gravesite, but I don't know what to do. I just can't go on or go back."

"Oh, please come go with us. The worst part of the journey is over," I lied. "The rains will soon let up. You can still get your photographs."

She was sitting in the backseat of our car even before she said yes. An Englishwoman. A short while later, we arrived in the small town of Hana, where we hoped to find beer and information, in that order. We found both in a bartender. He gave us the disturbing news that the distance to Kipahula was ten more miles. And he added, "The road really gets rough from here on."

I said, "That's like telling Lindbergh when he finally reached Paris that he had to go on to Rome." But what the Hana. We were there. The sun was now out. The scenery was incredibly incredible, and they had beer to go. So we went.

Our instructions were to look for a triple-tiered waterfall and then a red gate on the left. I had expected neon signs flashing "Lindbergh Buried Here." I should have known. We were in this remote place simply because Lindbergh had sought isolation and had found it on this windward side of Maui. He had wanted privacy and had gotten it, along with jungles, natural swimming pools, rumbling waterfalls, deep forests rich with mangoes and bananas, and the lonely Pacific. He had found his Shangri-la.

We found the gate. Had to climb over it, as a matter of fact. There was but a tropical trail bordered by coconut palms and wild plum and banana trees, leading us, we hoped, to the site of Lindbergh's grave. As we wandered down the trail, we encountered a couple coming our way—an elderly man and a handsome young woman holding his arm as they walked along. He greeted us with a big smile and "I'll bet you're looking for Lindbergh's gravesite."

I said, "Come to think of it, by golly we are."

"Well, when the trail forks stay to the left. This will lead you to a little white church and a graveyard near a huge banyan tree. You'll see a large rectangular grave that is Lindy's grave. He designed it himself. There are some smaller markers by it. These are markers of the graves of some gibbons. Lindy and I raised these blonde apes."

"That's a coincidence," I said. "A man with whom I work in radio and television has a gibbon ape."

"Oh, I'd dearly love to talk to you about that. You can see the roof of my house through the trees there. Why don't you folks come over and visit me when you're finished?"

We readily agreed to do that. We went our way. And as we rounded a turn in the trail, we came upon a scene that will forever be a part of us. Cascading down from three different consecutive heights were the waterfalls that we had been told to look for. There's a dollhouse of a church, the Pallapala Ho'omau Congregational Church built by Protestant missionaries in the 1850s. Typically Hawaiian with white plastered sides and a bright green roof, it sat peacefully in the shade of the meandering banyan tree. Nearby was the churchyard cemetery . . . all this on a high plateau overlooking the Pacific. Yes, the drive was worth it.

Now I knew why Lindbergh had told his doctors when death was near that he'd rather live a day in Maui than a month in New York. This is why he took his last flight and came back here from New York to die and to be buried.

And there was Charles Lindbergh's gravesite. A large rectangle of polished stones protected from the sun by wild plum trees. In the middle, a heavy slab of granite on which was carved:

Charles Lindbergh
Born Michigan 1902. Died Maui 1974.

And below, the biblical verse:

If I take the wings of the morning and
dwell in the uttermost part of the sea.

At the corners of the rectangular plot, small headstones mark the graves of Lindy's beloved apes.

At last I had come to the man I had so admired. As an amateur flier, I had flown those sleepy hours with Lucky Lindy in the *Spirit of St. Louis*. I was his co-pilot on those early, first days of airmail. I had bailed out with him when weather would not allow a landing. I, with the world, had grieved with him and his wife when their baby was kidnapped. And here, on this mystical plateau, I had come to his final landing on this Earth.

I described the scene, our feelings, our thoughts on my tape recorder, for my radio audience back home. Then we walked through the jungle to the nearby home of our new friend. A stalk of bananas hung on his front porch, but a short distance from its source.

"Oh, I'm so glad you decided to come over. We don't get to see many people around here. Here, sit down, sit down and make yourselves comfortable."

We did. "You can see the top of the Lindberghs' house right through there. I convinced him and Anne to come to Maui. I knew they would love it. And they did. I sold them the five acres on which they built their house. Yes, Lindy and I loved gibbons. See that black lava horseshoe-shaped beach down there? When he knew that his time was running out because of the cancer, he'd sit down there hour after hour in a folding beach chair, holding one of the apes in his lap, looking out to sea. Just looking out to sea. So your friend has a gibbon ape, too, eh? That is a coincidence. Say, I haven't introduced myself. My name is Pryor. Sam Pryor."

"Well, Mr. Pryor, we've got another coincidence working here. My name is Pryor, too."

"My goodness," the elder Pryor exclaimed. "My folks originally came from the Carolinas. How about yours?"

"Greenville, South Carolina."

"Incredible. Oh, I'm not minding my manners. My companion here is my nurse. [I don't recall her name.] At my age, I need a little help just being here, and she gives me a wonderful hand. And here's another important member of the family, my Labrador retriever. I love Labs as well as apes."

"Mr. Pryor, I don't want you to think I'm making all of this up, but I raise and train Labrador retrievers."

We were brought cooling drinks as we sat on the porch enjoying the company and the sight and fragrance of bougainvillea and hibiscus.

"You know, Mr. Pryor," I said, "I've been thinking today of Lowell Thomas, the famous news commentator and traveler. He was such a fan and supporter of Lindbergh. And our journey up here was the type of adventure that Thomas seemed to cherish."

"Well, not very far through the trees over there is a house owned by Lowell Thomas' son, Lowell, Jr. He married my daughter Mary."

The Englishwoman said, "I'm hearing all these incredible coincidences, and I can't believe my ears."

"No," continued Sam Pryor, "We don't get many visitors here. It's rather difficult to get to."

"Yes!"

"I do have a visitor coming next week from Texas. A dear friend who is the widow of a man I spent many pleasant hours with. She lives in Austin, Texas."

"Here we go again, Mr. Pryor. My wife and I live in Austin, Texas. Who is your friend?"

"Lady Bird Johnson."

Jewell and I looked at each other and then burst out laughing.

"Did I say something funny?"

"No, Mr. Pryor. But here is my business card. You can read for yourself. I work for radio station KLBJ . . . and you know who those initials stand for. Lady Bird Johnson."

We all stood speechless for a moment. Here on this tiny dot of lava in the middle of all this blue that covers so much of this small globe, but a tiny fraction of a great galaxy, the scattered lives of two of the five billion inhabitants of this planet melded for awhile in an incredible singleness.

After we had searched unsuccessfully for family ties that are bound to be there somewhere, our host said, "You had better be going along or plan to spend the night. You don't want to be on that road in darkness."

Immediate concurrence. We left reluctantly. Many stories untold . . . this reunion of two who had never met, who would never meet again.

We drove the Englishwoman back to her car. Her nerves, like the weather, now calm. The road had been repaired, and the trip back to the other side of Maui was uneventful except for the eventful scenery now not marred by clouds and rain and fear.

Later, back home in Texas, I learned more about Sam Pryor. Samuel Frazier Pryor, Jr., as vice president and director, was one of the early leaders of Pan American Airlines. As vice president of Pan American World Airways, he had traveled this globe over while establishing airports. He personally knew almost every leader of the nations to which airplanes flew, including Franklin Roosevelt, Harry Truman, Lyndon Johnson, Tojo, Benito Mussolini, and Adolf Hitler. Lady Bird and Lyndon

Johnson's friend was once vice chairman of the Republican National Committee and was in charge of Wendell Wilkie's East-
ern Headquarters in the 1940 presidential campaign. During
World War II, he found locations for the Allies' landing strips
around the world. When he retired from Pan American, he came
back to his favorite spot on the globe he had traveled so exten-
sively . . . back to Maui. He owned considerable land on the
island. He is dead now, as is my wife, Jewell.

I will go back on that road . . . to Kipahula and to Lindy's
grave. It is a place of great magic, and it calls loudly.

ELEVEN

I Am You

y dear late friend, humorist, and civil-rightist John Henry Faulk planted the seed in my mind. We were walking on Austin's beautiful hike and bike trail during the latter days of his life. It was one of those mornings that makes you want to hold onto life forever.

John Henry said, "You know, Cactus, I am part of all this. I am at one with those bass making circles out there in the lake and those ducks coming in for a landing. I am at one with my Chinese brothers, my German brothers, with people of all races and colors and with that moon sinking below Mount Bonnell over there. I am at one with the universe."

A few years later, I recalled Johnny's words during that incredible time when the world seemed to change overnight. The Berlin Wall came down. The Soviet Union surrendered communism and unshackled millions of people. The Free World bonded together to deal with corrupt dictators who stole food from starving masses. It was a return to that which inspired this nation . . . a sense of dignity for the individual. A recognition of the specialness, the uniqueness of each and everyone of us. And yet, despite our universal distinctiveness, we are all the same. We are all passengers on this incredible space ship called Earth. We are all riders on Walt Whitman's Brooklyn Ferry: "Just as any of you is one of a living crowd, I was one of a crowd."

I delivered the following commentary for my Christmas broadcast:

I am you and you are me.

I cry, you cry. I laugh, you laugh. I hunger, you hunger. The wind that brought the bogeyman outside my rattling window brought him outside your flapping desert tent or your shaking palm leaf hut.

We all run to mother when we are hurt.

We come back to where we began . . . to that wonderful, familiar, soft safety.

And we all look to father to protect us and feed us, even though sometimes mother is father, also.

And sometimes father is mother, also.

And when they are no longer here for us to run to, we become the haven for our children to run to.

We all seek another . . . for love . . . for comfort . . . for the sweetness of sharing. And if we don't have that, we hurt for not having it, especially if we had it and have lost it.

We look at the stars, and we wonder . . . how far? How many? And who put it all there? And will we go there? Anywhere? And why? Why us? Why here? Why now? And when will we leave? And will I be afraid? Will it be peaceful?

And what will you do when I am there, and you are here?

Or you are there, and I am here?

Sometimes I smell the flowers; sometimes I can't.

Sometimes I like you.

Sometimes I don't.

Sometimes I am sad and don't know why.

John Henry Faulk and friend. Photo by Bill Leissner.

Sometimes I am happy and don't know why.
Sometimes I lose me and wonder if I will ever find me.
Sometimes I am full of me . . . sick of me . . . tired of me . . .
joyous of me . . . proud of me . . . ashamed of me.
Sometimes I even like me.
I soar, I fall. I sing, I cry. I succeed, I fail.
But I am not alone . . .
for I am you and you are me.
So are we all.
And we are all special, for we are here.
If we were not, we would never have been here . . .
This wonderful, painful, glorious, sorrowful, magnificent here.

TWELVE

Death in Louisville

f course, I was in love with Phyllis George. Wasn't every red-blooded American male who would have given up a passing grade in algebra for a date with this former Miss America? "Boy, she's not only the most beautiful woman in the world, this gal also knows football! Talks about it on the TV. Holds her own with Jimmy the Greek and them guys. I mean, this gal's got class!"

I first fell in love with Phyllis when I emceed her homecoming in Denton, Texas, after she was chosen Miss America. Later I shared other events with her, including a convention show in San Diego. She'll never forget San Diego. Our hosts took us to Sea World. The emcee invited her to come down to poolside and look into the water. Whereupon a killer whale emerged and did what all American men wanted to do, kissed Phyllis George, sending her into near hysterics.

So when I received a phone call from Phyllis asking me if I would come to Kentucky and emcee the inaugural gala of her governor husband John Y. Brown, I died and went to heaven . . . and heaven was in Louisville, Kentucky.

She informed me that some of the people whom I would introduce and who would be entertaining were Kentuckians Muhammad Ali, Andy Williams, actor Lee Majors, and comedian Foster Brooks. Wow! She suggested that I include some of my funny stuff.

Never have I so wanted to knock 'em dead. I had to. Phyllis was kind enough to invite a fellow Texan to participate in one of the big moments of her life. I had to justify her choice. Kentucky had given Texas Jim Bowie; now Texas will give you Cactus Pryor! I called her secretary. I told her I wanted topical subject matter. Inside stuff that the Kentuckians could identify with. Names, situations. Anything I could turn into a gag. I then did something I've never done before. I borrowed material from my dear friend, humorist John Henry Faulk. Johnny had some original political gags that were surefire with any political audience, that is, when he delivered them. John Henry was a storyteller. I am a one-liner man. But, for Phyllis, I'd switch for one night.

It was a high-toned evening. I was given my own limousine and driver, who would be at my command during my entire stay in Louisville. I was privileged to have a special invitation to the swearing-in of the new governor immediately following the gala. It was a black-tie and white linen banquet. I was seated next to Muhammad Ali's beautiful wife. A large orchestra with more violins than had ever been assembled in one place in Kentucky played background music. The meal looked incredible. I wished I could have talked my nervous stomach into accepting it.

After the meal, I was introduced to the audience as Phyllis' good friend from her native Texas. "Cactus Pryor is one of the funniest guys around." Yeah . . . me and Dr. Jack Kavorkian.

I bombed. Not a ten-ton bomb. A big time, class A, major-major, all-time mega hydrogen bomb. The "inside" material was so inside no one knew what I was talking about. And John Henry Faulk's material did not compute with a Pryor delivery in the

With Phyllis George.

state of Kentucky. As I spewed out line after line to a dead-silent audience, my mouth was as dry as El Paso. I was fighting hyperventilation but at the same time hoping I would pass out, anything to get outta there. I staggered through the introductions. The entertainers were hailed like heroes by the audience, hungry for relief from me. I had more to say, but one of the committee members decided it would be more appropriate if a member of the committee finished the remaining amenities.

Yeah . . . and Kentucky Fried Chicken Governor Brown would like to talk to me about being fried.

I did not attend the swearing-in ceremony. I did not take my limousine back to my hotel. I walked the three miles in rain and sleet. "Go ahead. Hit me in the face. Freeze me. I deserve it." I did not wait to fly back the next evening. I took the first plane home to Austin.

It took me years to recover. Hell, I still haven't. I wrote this as a catharsis, but it ain't working. But I had a chance to redeem myself recently. It was a huge celebration of Lady Bird Johnson's eightieth birthday. The large auditorium in the LBJ Library was the site of a gala. There were VIPs galore. From Bill Moyers to the Laurance Rockefellers. I was the master of ceremonies. I had been told that Phyllis George would be in the audience. Another chance!

And I wowed them. Every gag was a three-bagger. Yeah! You see, Phyllis? I really am a funny guy. Now you know I only had an off night in Kentucky.

When I went to find her during the dinner that followed, I was told, "Phyllis didn't make it."

Argggggh!

THIRTEEN

Joshua's Shoes

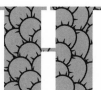e saw it on television. He saw the basketball player of the century bend over and pump up his shoes. He saw the icon jump to an amazing height far above the basket and then slam-dunk the ball with the ease of a ballet dancer. He returned to the floor yards below with the lightness of a feather drifting down. Joshua wanted a pair of those basketball shoes.

Joshua has a great future as a salesman. He talked the family into mortgaging their home to float a loan, adding the money they'd saved for his college career, selling their pet dog so that they could pay for a pair of those shoes. But these were not ordinary shoes. Cinderella would have killed for a pair of these shoes. Unlike her slippers, these shoes not only could be pumped up, they could also be deflated. And unlike Cindy's shoe, they would stay on your feet.

After buying the shoes, Joshua chose not to wear them until he had mastered the magic. He carefully examined them. He

47

noted the pump. It came in the configuration of a small basketball on the top of each shoe. He remembered how his basketball god had done it on the television commercial. He pushed down on the basketball. He could hear the swish of air going into the shoe. Again he pumped . . . and again. Yes, the shoe was inflating! Then he tried the deflating. The whoosh of air escaping told him that deflation was in progress. Joshua practiced and practiced the inflating and deflating process until he felt ready to wear the shoes. He called the family in to witness the launching of their investment. Proudly he donned them. They gasped as he pumped air into them and grew taller and taller. They oohed and aahed as he released the air. Their one remaining dog barked, startled by the noise. Again Joshua pumped up his shoes. Then he jumped.

Although but five feet six, his head brushed the top of the ceiling. Olajuwon, beware!

Every night before he went to bed, Joshua would deflate his shoes. One simply does not retire for the night with one's shoes inflated. Throughout the day, he would call the Weather Bureau to learn the proper barometric pressure of the hour for proper adjustment of the pressure in his shoes.

Joshua traveled with his family to the coast for a holiday. Before leaving he acquired a map listing the various altitudes they would encounter along the way. Several times during their journey, they stopped the car so Joshua could inflate or deflate his shoes. Joshua wanted to be altitudinally correct.

One day while at the coast, the family rented a boat for a fishing trip. They went miles out to sea seeking the big ones. When a dark wall of clouds began building on the horizon, Joshua's father decided to head for the harbor. But the motor would not start. The storm grew nearer and nearer as the father frantically pushed the starter button to no avail. The wind hit with a blast of wet air. Their boat was tossed around at the will of the wind and the waves that were taking them further and further out to sea. Even if they should survive the storm, they would be stranded at sea without food and water. They were at extreme risk.

While the other members of the family frantically bailed water out of the boat, Joshua began pumping up his shoes. He pumped and pumped until his fingers were numb. The shoes reached a poundage of air for which they were never intended. The wind was now at its peak. Through the sheets of rain, the family could barely see a platform on which an oil derrick stood. Oh, to reach that haven. But no chance. The wind and currents were taking them away from it. Then Joshua went forward, took the bow rope in hand, and stepped onto the water.

"Joshua, what are you doing? You'll drown!" Oh, ye of little faith. Joshua walked across the surface of the tossing sea, pulling the boat toward the platform. This young Baptist with only his basketball shoes to support him towed the boat bearing his precious family to the safety of this man-made gift from heaven. Several hours later, after the storm had subsided, the United States Coast Guard found Joshua and his family safely moored to the drilling platform.

Joshua and his magical shoes became legend in Redfield, Arkansas. He set a new state record for slam dunks for players under five feet seven inches. He won the Redfield Junior High School high-jump competition. Joshua followed the desire of his heart and started dating Bessie Lou Crawford. He had always loved her. But Bessie Lou was five feet ten inches tall. She would never consider dating one his height. But now, wearing his shoes, he could pump himself up to five feet ten and one-half. They were beautiful dancing together on the gymnasium dance floor, cheek to cheek.

Unfortunately, the story of Joshua and his shoes cannot be concluded. We do not know the ending. Joshua took a commercial flight from Little Rock to Memphis, where he was to play the role of a hippity-hoppity rabbit in an Easter pageant. We don't know exactly what happened but the FAA reported the incident thusly:

"At 10:00 A.M. on April 1, 1994, Trans-Continental Air Flight Number 67 departed Little Rock, Arkansas, for Memphis, Tennessee. The plane was assigned an altitude of 24,000 feet. Upon reaching its assigned altitude, the plane continued to ascend. When questioned by the traffic controller, the pilot reported that the plane was continuing to rise on its own. His controls were ineffective. The plane reached an altitude of 40,000 . . . then 50,000 feet. At the height of 200,000 feet, it disappeared from the radar screen. However, voice contact with the pilot remained intact. His last call reported an incredible altitude that was beyond the gravitational pull of Earth. He reported all systems were working other than his controls for ascent or descent. Gradually radio contact faded away."

That was the official report from the FAA. Occasionally, however, ham radio operators report receiving a faint voice contact from Trans-Continental Flight Number 67, too garbled to understand.

If you should be listening to this radio report, Joshua, deflate!

FOURTEEN

The Net Caster

ed up with watching football on the tube, I left our friends' condominium on Mustang Island and sought the serenity of the tidal flats in nearby Corpus Christi Bay. I took my casting net with me, hoping to catch enough mullet to do some surf fishing. It was midafternoon, and most fishermen had already retreated to watch the Dallas Cowboys play whomever they were playing. And I thought, hooray for the Cowboys. They have given me some solitude. I had rather watch the long-billed curlews in their contest against crabs and worms and hear their cheers, "cur-lewwwww . . . cur-lewwwww." I had rather feel the tug of a fish than the shove of the crowd.

There was one man sharing the day with the always busy sandpipers, gulls, and flights of brown pelicans, thankfully back again in profusion after nearly meeting extinction before preservation methods paid off. He was poling a small, obviously homemade pirogue-type boat down a channel. As he approached me, he grounded his boat and unloaded what appeared to be a plastic garbage container on wheels. It also supported an aerator of some sort. His boat held a number of similar containers. Obviously this man was after a lot of bait. He then slung a casting net over his shoulder and set out wading across the shallow tidal flats as a disorganized flight of cormorants, winter Texans, flapped overhead.

I had been casting my net for fingerling mullet for several hours and had but a mere dozen for my efforts. A stout wind created ripples on the water that made the illusive bait fish almost impossible to see, even with Polaroid glasses. So I was interested in learning if this fellow would have better luck than I.

On his first cast of the huge net, I knew I was watching a professional. A big man . . . six feet four inches or so . . . around 240 solid pounds . . . linebacker size. He cast the lead-weighted net with the ease of Troy Aikman throwing a down-and-out to Michael Irvin. Most of us right-handed amateurs attach the net's rope to our left wrist. We then lift the skirt of the net and spread it out between the right and left hands. When we toss the net, we give it a twirling motion that we hope will unfold and land it on the water in a perfect circle. But this man put the rope on his right wrist, grabbed the top of the net with his right hand and threw it like a football. Every time he achieved the perfect circle. When he retrieved his first cast, I could see that the net was full of fish. He emptied them with practiced ease into his container. He moved a few yards . . . watched the water patiently, ever so like a huge blue heron, and then cast his net again. Even into a stout wind, into which you never toss a net, it was another perfect cast. Again, the net came back full of mullet.

When he finally waded toward a saltwater-weathered pickup bearing a huge sign reading FISH, I approached him.

"Mister, you are some artist."

"What's that?" he responded with a big smile.

"I said you are some kind of artist with that net. You must do this for a living."

"I do," he replied. "Well, kind of a living. I also fish and guide."

I said, "I noticed that you tie your rope to your right wrist and hold the net differently from anyone I've ever seen. Would you show me your technique?"

I realized that I was asking Ben Crenshaw to show me his putting stroke. But he said, "Sure thing."

He then spent about fifteen minutes instructing with amazing patience a very inept student. I said, "But you are seeing the mullet even when they're invisible."

"Well," he drawled, "after awhile you learn to think like they do."

After he concluded that I had learned about all I was going to learn about throwing the castnet, he said, "Well, gotta get back to my work" . . . and so he did.

I lingered awhile longer just to watch this expert doing well the job he loves.

I think of him often when the deadlines overwhelm, the telephone overrings, the bank account overdraws . . . and especially when Aikman overthrows for an interception.

FIFTEEN

The Panhandle Pundit

marillo, Texas, is a city of 160,000 people surrounded by Stanley Marsh 3. Geographically, the Panhandle city is closer to the capitals of five other states than to its own Texas capital in Austin. This puts five states in greater risk from Stanley Marshisms than Texas. At risk, that is, if you have a lack of appreciation for true, pure-dee, unbridled, refreshing originality. To say Stanley Marsh is an original (he angers when called an eccentric) is as understated as saying that Adolf Hitler was tacky.

Driving the vast prairieland that is the Texas Panhandle has been described as driving miles and miles of nothing but miles and miles. However, Stanley Marsh has changed this. Depending on the direction from which you are traveling, you might first encounter Stanley's creative bent when, "My God, Maude. Lookie yonder. There's a giant cow patty floating over the top of that mesa!"

And from another direction, "Maude, I'll kiss a mule if there ain't ten Cadillac cars buried nose down in that field over there. Am I going crazy, or am I really seeing that?"

Yes, dear traveler, you are seeing another Stanley Marsh surprise on Marsh's Cadillac Ranch, "Stonehenge for America."

Flying in, if you pass over the city of Amarillo and look down upon the business section, "Maude, look down there. Right over to the right there. There's a flying saucer that landed right square dab in the middle of the town. Look at them blinking lights."

And he's right, Maude. Except this flying saucer doesn't fly. And inside you'll not find aliens but employees of Marsh's highly successful ABC television station.

Drive out from town in another direction, and "Maude, would you look at that? That windmill is yellow and is wearing a bow tie. What kind of town is this, Maude?"

It's where Stanley Marsh 3 was born and lives and chooses to stay, Maude. If someone put a pistol to his head and said, "Get out of Amarillo or I'll pull this trigger," Stan would reply, "What caliber pistol is that?"

Son of a wealthy oilman, Stan has amused, confused, inspired, and entertained the good citizens of Amarillo since birth. And made some of them damn mad, too. An Amarillo friend of his told me that Stanley Marsh enjoys being controversial. That if everyone loved all that he does, then he wouldn't do it.

My wife, Peggy, and I visited this Texas Panhandle legend to tape a radio interview with him. Fortunately, the tape recorder malfunctioned, and we had to return to Amarillo to repeat the interview. It requires at least two visits with Stanley Marsh to realize that he is not someone you dreamed up, like Dorothy in Oz.

He drove us to the floating mesa in his London taxicab and explained the optical illusion that you can spot from eleven miles away. The land on which the phenomenon is perpetrated is partially owned by his wife, Wendy. Stanley erected a metal fence 8 feet tall and 250 feet long about 10 feet below the crest of the rise. It is painted a very light blue color. During certain times of the day when the weather is right, the top of the mesa appears to float as the fence blends in with the sky. It has been viewed as a flying saucer, a lake, or as Marsh labels it, "A giant cow patty in the sky."

Then we drove to the Cadillac Ranch. The ten Cadillacs buried nose down symbolize the American dream of going to California. Later he painted them pink to make them girl Cadillacs . . . "Like the pretty girls who go to Hollywood and are discovered and become movie stars and get rich and then move back to Amarillo."

Why? Why Cadillac sculptures and floating cow patties?

"You play with the toys you have. Wendy and I live in an area where there's a great deal of land and very few people. Because I'm lucky to have access to a lot of this land, our toys are of a larger scale than if we lived in an apartment in Manhattan or in Austin, where land is so valuable."

Amarillo suits him. He was born there in 1938. As he drove us around his town, he proudly pointed out the features and character of the community. He revels in this West Texas city where they had to import yuppies just for show and would have to bring in a trust officer from out of town to write a family trust.

"The Texas Panhandle is a place where a lot of good people live, and most of them are ornery, tough, mean, opinionated, and smart. When the Dust Bowl and the Depression came along, the nice ones all left and moved out to the San Fernando Valley. Only the ornery stayed. That's what makes it so nice. The people here earned the right to stay here. They deserve the right to be called pioneers because they toughed it out."

Stanley claims he doesn't march to a different drummer. That's because he invented the marches. He describes himself as "an average Amarillo citizen, middle-aged, middle-class, middle American. And it's wonderful to get to stay where you grew up and to like it and have a good time there, and I think that a lot more people are like that than we know."

He married the right woman. Wendy has always enjoyed Stanley doing his own thing, including wearing a gorilla cos-

Interviewing Stanley Marsh 3. Photo by Peggy Davis Pryor.

tume in Africa and climbing Mount McKinley in Alaska at the age of forty-three dressed as a Boy Scout. She is a lawyer, born in Amarillo, and is very involved in the community. Her grandfather was working for his father-in-law, Joseph F. Glidden, when Glidden invented barbed wire. Toad Hall, the small ranch where the Marsh family now resides, was once headquarters for a ranch of over two hundred square miles. Wendy's grandfather then proceeded to fence in the entire awesome acreage, thus introducing barbed wire to the Texas Panhandle. It was, also, the first ranch in the world to be completely enclosed with barbed wire. Besides being a working cattle ranch, Wendy's land, as well as a portion of Stanley's family's land, holds a good part of the world's largest helium dome. It must keep the natives awake at night wondering what Stanley Marsh might do with that lighter-than-air stuff.

The Marshes live in a rambling ranch house on the outskirts of Amarillo. They have five adored adopted children who grew up with a bright yellow windmill that wears a neon bow tie at Christmas time. Of course the place is called Toad Hall.

When we visited their home, we couldn't help but notice a Volkswagen buried nose down on the front lawn. Stan's brother and friends have a bizarre sense of humor, too. We also couldn't help asking, "Stan, what's the purpose of those large red, yellow, and blue letters leaning against the backyard fence?"

"You'll notice the letters are *A, R,* and *T.* That's the answer to the age-old question of man, 'What is art?' Well, there's the answer. That's art."

Of course they have a prairie dog village on their property. What would a Toad Hall be without prairie dogs? Naturally they had what was probably the largest white horse in America grazing happily around their property . . . now grazing in that great green pasture in the sky. And spread generously around their property, old farm equipment has been fashioned into dinosaurs. Somehow we were not surprised to discover in Stanley's twelfth-story office suite in downtown Amarillo a full-sized croquet court on Astroturf. "Everyone should have one."

Life in Amarillo with Stanley Marsh is like living with a jack-in-the-box. You never know when and where and what will pop up next. He doesn't refer to these Marshisms as gifts to Amarillo. "I am an elitist. I do these things because I enjoy them. I hope that other people will enjoy them, like what I like . . . and I like to be popular. But I didn't do it for applause but because I wanted to. I have made a system of unanticipated rewards . . . surprises that people see where they don't expect to see them . . . things that happen to you when you walk into a rose garden and go around a corner, and there's a surprise and no anticipation."

His latest surprise, incidentally, is art in the form of signs painted to look very much like official street signs. Imagine driving along and at the intersection of Bonham Street and Interstate 40 spotting a diamond-shaped yellow sign with black lettering reading, "Road Does Not End." This prompted a letter from the Amarillo Traffic Engineer informing Marsh of the illegality of erecting private signs on street rights of way. Stanley responded as a representative of the Dynamite Museum, formerly the anonymous organization called The Secret Society without a Name. He wrote that the Dynamite Museum is "distressed that it was not informed that the ART was being removed." He added that the museum took exception to the traffic engineer's reference to their ART as signs.

The ART continues popping up, making the streets of Amarillo, Texas, perhaps the most artistic in the United States. On Hughes Street, one sees a white cat and a black cat prowling on two yellow diamond-shaped signs, er, metal canvases. On Danbury Street, there is a "Dinosaur X-ing." Marilyn Monroe stands facing . . . you got it . . . Monroe Street between Eighth and Ninth Avenues. And at Eleventh and Polk, drivers are greeted by Mona Lisa, "Men Have Loved Her."

We received a letter from Stanley one day. The postman brought it to the door, for it was too long to fit into the mailbox. Of course.

Want to feel better about being an American? Spend some time with Stanley Marsh 3. He's a patriot.

He loves children. That's because there's so much child in the man. His eyes sparkle when he talks about his projects. An impish grin consumes his whole face as he unveils yet another wild scheme.

Marsh 3 makes Amarillo . . . and wherever he may be . . . come alive. He is Barnum and Bailey with a dash of Buffalo Bill Cody, a dab of Andy Warhol, and more than a smidgen of Peter Pan. He's usually seen wearing a bright yellow shirt, a two-quart white Panama, and tennis shoes on constantly moving feet.

"Stanley," I asked him, "What do you fear?"

"Risking my life. I'm opposed to premature death. I dislike pain. And I'm afraid of my ice cream melting and dripping on my yellow shirt."

What next? Well, I promised not to tell, but don't panic if you're driving down the road to Tucumcari and suddenly see the head of a full-sized adobe sphinx peeking at you from behind a tall mesa.

As I interviewed Stanley, for some reason there came to mind the circles in the wheat fields of England near Stonehenge.

SIXTEEN

Gift to George

e took George with us on our honeymoon . . . at least in thought. We knew that he would have so enjoyed the sights. And that's why Peggy and I were driving up that scary road that encircled that mountain like a coiled up South Texas rattlesnake. The shoulders bordered drop-offs that spelled curtains. You quickly learned to look straight ahead. Peggy, a world-class second-seat driver, was unusually silent. Ominously our rent-a-car was labeled Alamo. We were praying that these two Texans would not be joining David Crockett and William Travis.

We were climbing to the top of Kauai . . . the garden island of the Hawaiian chain. It is noted for its deep canyons and lush growth. At the moment, we were on the southwestern side of the island. Our journey was taking us to a spot where we could look down on those canyons with dry palms. We were going there for George.

George is a rancher. A brush country rancher. Brush country ranchers are different than other Texas ranchers. They're tougher and often hungrier. They're more mesquite than oak, more beef jerky than tenderloin. They move constantly among thorns. They can't talk five minutes without using the word "drought" at least once. They recall the terrible drought at the turn of the century when the Baptists were taking to sprinkling, the Methodists were using a wet rag, and the Episcopalians were handing out rain checks. When it was so dry, the bushes were whistling at the dogs. George says that every year they have a two-year drought down in McMullen County. He sings a song he wrote about his daddy. They took him to a picture show in San Antonio. In the film, it was raining almost constantly. Probably was shot in England. George says his dad sat through that show three times just to watch it rain. They had to bring him back again a few days later, so he could watch it rain again.

George lives for the prospect of rain. His future is based on the hope for rain. He knows if it rains he's going to have a better chance of buying that part he needs for his old pickup or for his antique tractor. He knows if it rains he might be able to make a payment on the note that he signed for the money with which to buy some more cows. George watches two shows daily on television: the six o'clock weather and then the ten o'clock weather, hoping that there has been a change in the forecast during those four hours. And that's why Peg and I were driving up that skinny road on a small island out in the middle of the Pacific Ocean.

Finally, we reached our destination . . . the top of the mountain. There was a small observation park on a narrow ridge. To our left, a broad sweep of blue Pacific; to our right, the canyons of Kauai. Grand ones like in Arizona.

Hanging over the greenery and lava rocks that prelude the Pacific was a rainbow. The mother of rainbows, for they say it goes away only at night and returns with the sun every morning. We yearned for Judy Garland.

Then, straight ahead, there it was . . . through the mist and clouds. This one's for you, George. The wettest spot on Earth.

An average of 451 inches of rain a year. Compare that to your 18 to 40 inches a year, if that much, in McMullen County. We took a picture of the sign so identifying this remarkable site. We snapped dozens of other shots of the rain.

Then we sent the pictures to George with this note: "When the grass burns away down there on your South Texas ranch . . . and the tanks dry up and you have to haul water and take a blow-torch to burn the thorns off the prickly pear so your cattle can eat . . . take a look at these pictures, George, of the wettest spot on Earth . . . and know that, though not in McMullen County, there is one place where it is raining."

SEVENTEEN

Lufkin Man

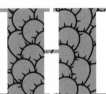is briefcase read "Lufkin, Texas," and his face read fatigue. The man in the Miami International Airport that Sunday at 6:30 A.M. had obviously been flying a long journey. But he was ready to talk about it. "Been down in Argentina." His accent said Lufkin, Texas, too. "Boy, will I be glad to get home to Momma and some home cooking. They eat a lot of meat down in Argentina . . . 'specially in Buerno Air-rus. It's good beef, but 'bout all they do is fry it. Not chicken fry . . . just fry it on a grill or in a frying pan. I've been flying all night. I tell you, when they invented them airplane seats, they didn't have my body in mind. And I've fed better food to my hogs. First thang I do when I get into my pickup at the Houston Airport is head for a little restaurant about sixty miles down the road to Lufkin that has beans and cornbread. Cornbread is the staff of my life. I figure if the Lord hadn't intended for us to eat cornbread he wouldn't have put it here."

He has a garden, he told me. Doesn't water it. "If the Lord

wants me to have vegetables, he'll provide the water. If he don't, he won't."

He spoke of things he loved with that possessive "my" that people who pride themselves in their work with their hands so often use. "My tamaters are doing good. My okra ain't. But my squash is." I imagine he used that same proud "my" when referring to his work tools . . . my wrench . . . my screwdriver.

He works for a company that manufactures pumps and other machinery. He'd been down to Argentina to work on an oil well pump that wasn't doing the job it was supposed to do and that the drillers hadn't been able to fix.

"Did you get it working again?" I asked.

"Oh, sure." This man, undoubtedly was good at his work.

"Do you always travel alone?"

"Most of the time," he replied.

"How many trips have you made out of the country?"

"A few."

"To where?"

"Oh, places like Afriker, Puerto Rica, the Virgin Islands, India, the Persian Gulf area, High-wi-ee . . . few places like that. I took Momma along last time I went to High-wi-ee. We stayed three weeks. Momma got island fever, and I was purty hungry for the piney woods of East Texas myself."

He spoke of some property they had bought. He was anxious to get home to see how a pond he had bulldozed out was coming along. He's planning to raise his own freshwater catfish to go with Momma's cornbread.

I don't know his name, but I know this man. I've known him many years and frequently in East Texas. He grew up with oil well machinery. He knows machines and makes his living fixing them. But he knows the land, too, and is close to it. Has to be. He's an evolutionary link between the man who planted with a stick and those who break the earth with mighty-motored tractors. He would prefer the simpler life, but he's made his peace with the machine age, too. He represents the best of both eras. And he's comfortable with himself . . . even in Miami Airport early on a Sunday morning after an all-night flight from Argentina.

EIGHTEEN

There Is Hope

he first comedy act I can remember was Grandma Pryor removing her upper plate and making a funny face at me. Excuse me, Grandma, for plagiarizing your bit.

Dad made us laugh with his jokes left over from his vaudeville days.

My first movie comedy hero must have been Charlie Chaplin. I was mesmerized by his ability to make people laugh with silly walks. All these years later, I can't get through a day without trying to capture a laugh with a silly walk. I giggle every time I remember the scene in the movie where he cooked his shoes and ate the laces as if they were spaghetti.

Then I discovered the irreverent humor of W. C. Fields, the slapstick of the Marx Brothers and the Three Stooges. I borrowed the styles of all of them in trying to make my friends and school-mates laugh. I had moderate success in achieving what I realized was a very important need in my life . . . to create laughter.

Will Rogers became my hero the first time I heard him on the radio. I was enthralled by his ability to take something from the daily newspaper and turn it into a gag. He influenced me much deeper than I could have imagined at that young age. Yeah! Make a joke about a person in the audience or about something of common knowledge. That's neat.

From elementary school to high school, I tried out the various forms of comedy that I admired. Civic Theater was a good boot camp and often as tough. I tried my wings at assembly programs at school, campfire shows at summer church camp. I shudder to recall some of the efforts and the pain when no one laughed. Once before a local civic club, I tried telling Will Rogers–like stories. It was not working. I hyperventilated and had to be carried to the kitchen for reviving.

And then I found God. I found Hope. He was the combination of all the comedians I had loved. The physical humor of the silent movie guys, the instant ad-libs of Groucho Marx, the topical humor of Will Rogers. But all done with one-liners. One-liners! That's my kind of humor. If one gag doesn't work, there's no need to hyperventilate. There's another one coming right after it that probably will work. Social security.

I discovered Hope on radio, then in the movies. While attending UCLA radio lab at the studios of NBC in Hollywood, I would sneak into the sponsor's booth and watch Hope and Crosby rehearsing their radio shows, hour after hour, cracking the crew up with only an occasional reference to the script. I was the most privileged peeping tom in the United States.

Bob Hope became my teacher. Air Corps squadron shows became my practice range. I borrowed not only his style but his being. I have a Hope nose. He's got an easy walk to copy. I do a good Hope voice. So I learned that I could garner laughs by coming on with the Hope walk singing "Thanks for the Memories" and throwing a few one-liner topical gags at the audience. I've always harbored a secret yearning to play Hope in a movie of his life. He's outlived a lot of younger actors who wanted to do that.

Like almost everyone who was born in the last three quarters of this century, I had the opportunity to meet Bob Hope. He joined Texas Governor Allan Shivers for a charity golf match in Austin. I asked for and won the honor of driving his golf cart. I even got to introduce him to the gallery. I drove the cart as carefully as if carrying a cargo of nitroglycerin. Now I had chance to learn the real Bob Hope, the serious side. I didn't find it. Throughout the eighteen holes, he told me joke after joke.

Years later a telephone call gave me that for which I had always longed. The opportunity to portray Bob Hope for Bob Hope. Tony Zoppi, a well-known Las Vegas publicist, returned to his native Dallas, invited me to be a part of the last vaudeville show to star Bob Hope. It would be a benefit for the performing arts at the Majestic Theater in Dallas, the signature theater of Interstate Theaters that offered one of the major vaudeville circuits in the Roaring Twenties.

Bob O'Donnell, who was imported to Dallas by owner Karl Hoblitzell, booked some of the biggest stars in showbiz for the stages of the Interstate circuit. In 1927 O'Donnell caught Hope's act at the Majestic Theater. He was impressed enough to recommend him to a major agent in New York. This resulted in a Broadway show for Hope. While there, he was signed to a contract with Paramount Pictures. So on this night of May 5, 1984, fifty-seven years later, Bob Hope was returning the favor that launched his career. The Last Vaudeville Show starring Bob Hope, dancer Joey Heatherton with a dance line of the world-famous, high-kicking Kilgore Rangerettes, Tony Dorsett and a number of other Dallas Cowboys in white tie and tails singing special lyrics written by Tony Zoppi to "Thanks for the Memories". . . and old vaudevillian song-and-dance man Skinny Pryor's somewhat giggly and dazed son Cactus as emcee.

Rehearsal started at noon the day of the show. A full pit orchestra was practicing as I arrived. My father's blood was pumping in rhythm to the tune. Hope came in around two o'clock. As he walked down the aisle chewing gum and cracking jokes, he didn't look like an octogenarian. He appeared young enough to play me, two decades younger, in a movie. As he gazed around, his eyes remembered. For a moment, he stood silently and let yesterday return, and it seemed to envelop him.

On the stage, Zoppi reintroduced me to my idol. Hope did exactly what he had done at the charity golf match in Austin. He pulled me to him and placed his ski nose against my ski nose and suggested we might have had the same father. I responded with one of my shorter one-liners, "Yeah." Later, "Gawd! My dog has a better vocabulary. Why didn't I tell him how important he had been in my life . . . that he was my lifelong mentor?"

Though he had had little sleep the night before, Hope stayed all afternoon for the rehearsal. He was in a nostalgic mood, remembering vaudeville days, sharing them with us, and, always, telling jokes.

The Majestic was beautiful that night. It glowed with its new facelift. It appeared fifty-seven years younger. The vaudeville music of the Dallas Jazz Orchestra flowed from the orchestra pit, enveloping a house filled with Dallas' finest, drifting up into the balcony, reaching higher to the sculptured ceiling, and seeping into the souls of all who remembered those magical days of vaudeville. And then as they struck up "Thanks for the Memories," I said, "This one's for you, Skinny Pryor," picked up a golf club, assumed my Bob Hope sassy walk into the spotlight, and strode across that magnificent old stage to the microphone.

I had 'em for a few minutes. They thought I was him. At least there was a collective gasp when I revealed the impostor. And I didn't hyperventilate.

The first half of the show was Joey Heatherton's. When she danced, simply the sexiest woman in America . . . as she was when she didn't dance. Only Hope could comfortably follow that act. A showstopper for an opener.

The Dallas Cowboys had a better line on the field than on the stage. But they brought down the house like it was a stadium.

Likewise the God-loving, devilishly high-kicking Kilgore Rangerettes, next to oil and Earl Campbell East Texas' greatest products.

Then I introduced my God. He was hot. He was loving it. He was back in vaudeville. He was repaying a debt. He was scheduled to do about forty-five minutes. An hour after his opening, he was still on.

His director was frantically trying to cue the orchestra and lights for different routines that Hope kept pulling out of the old theatrical trunk. He was, also, sharing old memories with the audience who realized they were watching theater history. Finally the director threw up his hands and said, "Let him go." And he did . . . and did . . . and did.

After the show, a glittering party was held in a nearby hotel. Hope showed up around midnight. At two in the morning, I surrendered to fatigue. As I left, Hope was standing near the door still telling jokes to a group of adorers. I should have stayed. The orchestra kept playing the old tunes in my head all night long.

Oh, by the way, Hope had not caught my impersonation. He was in his dressing room at the time. Oh, well, maybe next time.

NINETEEN

The Credit Card

eg says to me, "We need to cancel this credit card. We've had it for years and have never used it. And each year we have to pay a fifty-dollar renewal fee."

"Okay," says I. "Give them a call and cancel it."

She tried, but it wouldn't work. The nice lady with the credit card company told her, via long distance, that since the card bears only my name I would have to be the one to cancel it.

I called the 800 number and was soon talking to one of the nicest people I've ever met by telephone. Her voice would attract bees.

"My, Mr. Pryor . . . you've been with us since . . . let's see . . . why since 1981, and you've never missed an annual payment. We certainly would hate to lose you. By the way, do you realize some of the benefits you can receive from other companies simply by using our card?"

I admitted, "No, I don't."

She explained some of them to me, including trips around

the world at the price of a ticket from Minneapolis to St. Paul, rooms at hotels where they'd pay you to stay, and rent cars that you'd almost never have to return.

"Well, now," mused I. "My wife didn't tell about these. Let me talk to her again."

"I knew I shouldn't let you talk to that woman," Peg responded. "That woman could talk you out of your hair. I checked out these companies that were supposed to provide all the fringe benefits she mentioned. They were not nearly as luscious as she explained them to be on the phone."

So I placed a collect 1-800 call again to the credit card company. This time I got the second most friendly person I'd ever met on the telephone. She, too, was so interested in me . . . and was so appreciative of my long association with their company and my prompt payments that she just couldn't stand losing me.

But I stood firm and said, firmly, "No, I really do want to cancel."

She countered with yet another benefit of retaining their credit card. The whole world would be opened up to me. I realized that this woman was not going to cancel my credit card. So I went to the old single-wing reverse-around-left-end hidden-ball play.

"Madam, you have been very, very nice. I feel that you are a wonderful person and a good American who probably does not dip snuff nor kick chickens. I really do appreciate your concern for me and my welfare and how retaining your card would enhance my life. But I have to be perfectly frank with you. The truth is, my dear, I am being incarcerated for five years."

Total silence . . . then, "Oh, I am so sorry. Well, we'll keep your name on file, and we'll be sure and contact you five years from now. And sir, have a good stay."

Honest.

TWENTY

The Naming

t was a melding of the Cohens and the Pryors. First, the coming together of two families to witness and celebrate the joining in marriage of Julie Cohen and Dayne Pryor. This beautiful young lady whose ancestors came to this country to escape the persecution of the Russians. This handsome young man with Danish and British blood . . . and some of the Indian blood that flowed through the veins of a distant relative, Indian athlete Jim Thorpe.

Both the youngest of their families. Both being married for the first time. Both elated in the certainty that they had found the right mate for the rest of their lives.

But before the vows, the preludes. The homogenization of two families. Awkward at first. Strangers, soon to be in-law relatives, testing the waters to determine attitudes and personalities. But as the evening of rehearsal and celebration flowed, common denominators were discovered. A collective sense of humor prevailed. The joining was personified by the matriarchs of both families: Ethel Cohen, born in Russia while the czars still ruled; Mary Pryor, daughter of Danish immigrants, celebrating her eighty-eighth birthday. The two of them sitting side by side and gazing with wonderment at this gathering for which they were primarily responsible.

The toasts and stories, no one was excused, brought tears of emotions and tears of babies up much past their bedtimes.

The wedding ceremony was another melding of traditions and religions. The minister, a common friend of the bride and groom, John Henry Faulk. He had been properly ordained in order to perform the wedding of Dayne's sister, Kerry, a few years before. A South Austin Methodist standing under the chupah marriage canopy reciting traditional phrases of Jewish marriage ceremonies. The bride and groom delivered their own vows of their own convictions and desires. An Apache prayer was delivered with Johnny's South Austin accent. The shared glass of wine symbolized the years of sharing ahead. And then came the ritualistic stomping of the glass by the groom.

Then, three years later, another ceremony in Houston. On the day before Hanukkah, a naming. The giving of a Hebrew name to Julie and Dayne's daughter Elizabeth Jewell Pryor. She was named after a grandmother that she would never know. The ceremony took place at the home of Grandfather Leon and Grandmother Evelyn Cohen. Friends and relatives of both families had gathered for the occasion. Friends and relatives all too well known by Dayne. He had been stricken with a flu virus upon his arrival in Houston a few days earlier. He claimed he was more endangered by drowning in the gallons of chicken soup thrust upon him than from the virus.

Rabbi Jack Segal performed the naming ritual. The baby was held on a silk pillow by her mother. Her father was but an onlooker. Then Elizabeth was passed into the arms of the mother's mother . . . into the arms of my wife, whom the grandchildren call GrandPeggy . . . into the arms of her godparents, an aunt and an uncle . . . and finally into the arms of her great-grandmother Cohen. The haven of the family.

The rabbi explained the new names. Elanah, a tree that will bend with the wind and not break. Magalid, a precious jewel, a precious gift. Elanah Magalid, dressed in a beautiful pink smocked dress with pale lace trim, seemed fully aware of the importance of the ceremony. She seemed to be listening to every word. She was joyous.

The bread of life was broken and shared. A glass of wine was poured . . . the wine of celebration and joy, shared by mother and by child as the mother dipped her fingers into the glass and then touched the lips of her daughter.

Then, a Hebrew song of celebration . . . a prayer and a poem of the beauty of a child. And a feeling of thanksgiving for this child who personifies the joining of two families. We prayed for the joining of all families of the world.

Bless you, Elizabeth Jewell Elanah Magalid Cohen Pryor. And bless your new little sister, Marissa. Soon to receive her Hebrew names. Pecos, son of Dayne's brother Paul, said he wanted a Hebrew name, too.

TWENTY-ONE

Fish Oil

don't expect my fish stories to be believed. I don't believe others' fish stories, so why should I expect others to believe mine? However, this one is kings-ex. This one you can believe because it is true. Trust me.

Much of the navigation used by amateurs such as myself in the Gulf of Mexico off Port Aransas is provided by such companies as Texaco and Exxon. The oil and gas wells and the accompanying platforms are checkpoints. For example, about five miles straight out the channel from Port Aransas are two platforms called the stand pipes. You know that a heading of 120 degrees as you clear the jetties will get you there. Then if you travel due east from the stand pipes for another twelve miles or so, you come to another identification marker, what fishermen call the leaner. It is a gas well structure that does have the appearance of leaning. So, on returning from further out, when you reach the leaner, you know that a compass heading of due west will get

Aboard the Sea? Si! *Photo by Peggy Davis Pryor.*

you to the stand pipes . . . and from there a heading of 300 degrees will get you home.

On our first day of fishing one August, my wife and sons and I fished with fair results around the eighteen-miles-out leaning pipe. Oil well structures draw fish and are a bonanza to fishermen. We were getting an occasional king mackerel and green dolphin but nothing to write an essay about. So desiring faster action, we decided to head our little twenty-footer even further out into the deep blue, almost black, water of the Gulf to another marker on the far horizon. Thirty minutes later as we approached our destination, we saw that it was an oil derrick on a high platform.

Our heading, incidentally, from the leaning pipe had been 130 degrees. There we hit the honey hole. The king mackerel and the green dolphin (mahi mahi) were there and hungry. I renewed all my gasoline credit cards, for the workers on the oil rig high above us even directed us to fish that they could spot from their vantage point. Check your oil and tires, wipe your windshield, and spot your fish! The rig, by the way, was named *J. Storm X.*

So rewarded for our efforts, we decided to return to the rig the following day in our good ship the *Sea? Si!* Again we followed our homemade oil platform navigation procedure. Out the channel to the stand pipes . . . then to the leaner . . . then 130 degrees out to the *J. Storm X.* There was a haze that day, so visual sighting was limited. After thirty minutes at the same speed as the day before, on the same compass heading, the rig was still not in sight. We continued another fifteen or twenty minutes at the same heading. Thus far we had been to sea for two hours. Still no sighting.

Then my son Dayne spotted our destination, but much further north than expected. We assumed that we had miscalculated our compass heading, so off we went, going for the rig. We continued going for the rig and going for the rig and going for the rig. By now we must have been thirty-five to forty miles offshore, and I was beginning to wonder if any of those oil rigs had any gas for sale, for we were using a lot of it. As we closed in, we spotted three boats around the rig. Great! Boats usually mean fishing is good. Word quickly gets around on the fishing network. But wait a minute. The boats were not circling the rig as trolling boats usually do. They were . . . yes, towing the rig. As we got closer, we realized that the boats were tugboats. The rig was headed out to sea.

To shorten a too-long trip, we scooted back shoreward, found another oil platform . . . located more fish . . . and learned what lots of others have learned. You just can't count on the oil business in Texas anymore.

TWENTY-TWO

Great Britain and Texas
via Idaho

e discovered Great Britain while going down the Middle Fork of the Salmon River in Idaho. In the wildest stretch of U.S. wilderness, my son Dayne and I were introduced to the crooks and crannies of London. We found the heathered hills of the Scottish Highlands, the God-made golf links that separate the Atlantic and the North Sea from the tillable land of Scotland and England. In the heart of Idaho, we found the Hunters. The David Hunters of London, England . . . David, Julia, and their sons Alexander and Jeremy. And because they had come to this wild land to float the rapids that roar even higher than the English Channel in gales, the Hunters discovered Texas.

Illogical, the blending of Brits and Texans. Britishers are proper, in language, in manners. Always in control of the emotions. Always maintaining a certain dignity. Champagne with a swizzle stick. Sir Laurence Olivier.

Texans, wild and woolly. Irreverent, loud-mouthed, language-bashers, often shy of couth. Tequila on the rocks. Chill Wills.

No, not likely a melding of the Hunters and the Pryors on this journey. "My God! They even bathe every morning in the cold Salmon."

We became friends at the first laugh. Many would follow. We soon found common denominators . . . a spirit of adventure . . . a love of nature . . . a passion for fun . . . and a co-craziness.

We screamed through rapids that the outfitter had failed to mention in his brochure. "I say, Cactus, it appears that we are committed to navigating that alarmingly high rapids ahead. Is there an alternative?"

"Julia, just take a deep seat and get a faraway look in your eyes. We're coming out of chute number five on the buckingest bronco you ever straddled."

"Beg pardon?"

Juicy campfires with Texan Bob Armstrong picking and singing with his wife, Linda. Texas country songs and English ballads. Texas tall tales bringing giggles from young Shannon Armstrong and my son Dayne and snorts of disbelief from Alexander and Jeremy and chortles from David and Julia.

One twilight over cocktails, "Alexander, that mountain right across the river there. Would you mind climbing it to see if it offers a good view?"

I was kidding. Teenage Alexander wasn't. Without a word, he plunged into the icy stream. Thirty minutes later, he hailed us from the height of a mountain peak rapidly becoming unseeable because of darkness. Our guide with all the passion of a train schedule announcer said, "Hope he don't fall off that cliff to his right in the darkness. Rattlesnakes come out this time of night, too." He then sent his two sons to find Alexander in the gathering gloom. Alex found them. That same spirit of adventure has taken Alexander to India for charitable work, on a sailing schooner on a world voyage, and flying into Houston's jammed airspace in a single-engine plane.

The next time I challenged Alex was a year later at the Hunters' getaway home, Dounie, an hour's drive and a traditional Scotch whiskey toast to the Highlands north of Inverness, Scotland. We were having a picnic on a haunted hill where the rocks of a fortress built by a tribe of Picts during the Bronze Age surrounded us physically and metaphysically. The River Carron was rushing below, Salmon River–like. Though only early September, the air was for us Texans January chilly. "Alexander, I don't suppose you and Jeremy and your young friends would dare challenge that frigid pool of water below." Wherewith four young Brits stripped to their undershorts and screamed their way across the pool. Mad dogs and Englishmen.

It has become a homogenizing of cultures and places and affection. We have become a family separated only by the Atlantic and a common language. Dayne and I have introduced Jeremy and Alexander to the jumping green dolphin and fighting king mackerel of the Gulf of Mexico. They have vainly tried to introduce us to the salmon that allegedly swim up the River Carron. In the stream that flows through the land of the Hunter men's traditional college, Winchester College near the cathedral, we successfully avoided reducing the population of rainbow trout that are said to dwell therein.

While Bob Armstrong and I golfed with David and Julia at the consummate links course at Dornoch, Scotland, our dutiful wives, Peggy and Linda, prepared a meal of Texas Mexican food for which our British friends would give up tea and crumpets for life. The Hunters have even learned how to handle an explosive taco. We also positively introduced the Brits to grits. They in turn offered us one hundred different ways to prepare Scottish salmon. And David Hunter taught me . . . the hard way . . . to never . . . NEVER order high grouse in London's Buck Club. You'd think they'd at least clean the damn things.

The Armstrongs and the Pryors introduced the Hunters to golf in Texas, where white-tailed deer are official hazards. The Hunters introduced us to links courses with pot bunkers and gorse and winds that deserved to be named. I played my first game of golf on the other side of that great water hazard that is

David and Julia Hunter with Peggy and Cactus Pryor.

the Atlantic Ocean at proper Royal St. George's, next to David and Julia's home at Sandwich on the English Channel. Not knowing the proper decorum to be observed in royal golf clubs, I carefully observed my companions. On the first tee, David drove his ball out into the rough that was higher than tenderloin. Whereupon he muttered, "Drat, drat, drat!"

Alexander, sincerely troubled, responded with, "Father, get control of yourself."

I said, "Shit, I'm in trouble."

They have introduced me to wonderful interviews for my radio audience. Mr. Dye in his little shack in Sandwich. An aged man who served the royal family as their upholsterer and re-membered his fascination with the German zeppelins overhead during World War I . . . until they started dropping bombs. Kim Sawyer, the keeper of the estate at Dounie and a talented catcher of salmon and shooter of grouse. He surrendered the fast lanes of London for the serenity of the Highlands. Traded faxes for foxes.

Her majesty's kennel master and trainer of her Labrador retrievers at a field trial at the estate of the duke of Wellington. Tea with the duke of Marlborough at his London flat, touting for my radio audience his latest enterprise . . . tours of his lovely Blenheim Palace.

We introduced the Hunters to the two-step at the Broken Spoke in Austin, Texas. Tried to explain to them the rationale of everyone yelling out "Bullshit!" at the proper time when dancing the "Cotton-Eyed Joe." Watched them marvel at the sight of huge electric fans keeping putting greens cool. Watched Jeremy turn the hearts of University of Texas coeds and vice versa. Watched Alexander take a crash course in Texas law while working as an apprentice at Linda's law firm in Austin. And now he has become a barrister. Watched Jeremy become an addicted fan of the Dallas Cowboys with the proclivity to put his money where his mouth is. Anglophiles and Texanphiles.

Like Huck Finn, we learned that floating down a river on a raft is a wonderful way to know your traveling companions. To learn that color, geography, customs, economics, age, are but a beard. Shave it off and meet the real person underneath.

"Come float down the Middle Fork of the Salmon River in Idaho and discover Great Britain and the state of Texas and perhaps yourself."

Déjà Vu

have a feeling that I have written this before.

The 104-Year-Old Student

ecause his religion does not allow self-promotion, he asked me not to reveal his name. His age was documented as 104. A few months before I met him, he had had one of his legs amputated. Yet he lives alone in a house that has not weathered its years as well as he.

I came into his life because of a tip from a social worker friend who calls daily on the man. She suggested that he might make a fascinating interview for my radio audience. I took my tape recorder, but he would not allow me to record him. He did not think his church would approve. However, he did welcome a visit and conversation.

His memory of early life was fuzzy. Not because of the many years gone by, for he has excellent recall . . . but because he apparently was abandoned very early in life. He has no one with whom to share early life memories. He knew he was born on an Indian reservation in Florida. He remembers his mother marrying another man and leaving him as a very young child. He never knew his father.

Somehow, he wound up in San Antonio, Texas. He recalled living on the streets, parentless until he was about nine or ten. He had great difficulty in communicating with people. He spoke no English or Spanish at the time. His appearance was somewhat Hispanic. So when people spoke to him and he didn't respond, they dismissed him as being mentally deficient. Gradually, he picked up some understanding of English.

One day he spotted a mule-drawn wagon. On the seat was a loaf of bread. He stared at the bread with eyes filled with hunger. The wagon driver invited him to take the bread. The boy devoured it. The driver then asked the boy, "Do you have a father?"

He shook his head, no.

"Do you have a mother?"

Again, no.

"Do you have a place to live? . . . Then I will be your father and your mother." And the man swept the young boy up into a warm embrace, the first one he could remember receiving in his life. He took him to his ranch somewhere near San Marcos, Texas. He put the young man in charge of his livestock, mostly mules. He gave him a shack in which to live, far removed from the main ranch house. For about twenty years, he figured, his main companions were mules. He seldom saw any people.

At about thirty years of age, he decided he must find out about his mother. He left his shack and his mules, and he walked all the way from Central Texas to the Indian reservation in southern Florida. They told him they had no record of his mother. The chief scornfully informed him he was not a member of their tribe. He was not welcome. Heartbroken, he walked back to San Antonio.

He did not always live a lonely life. He told me he had been married six times. Only one of the wives gave him children. They are as scattered as his memories, and he does not hear from them. Tears came into amazingly bright eyes when he spoke of them.

Throughout many years, he earned his keep as a sheepherder in the mountain country ... Montana, Wyoming, Colorado, Idaho, Nevada, and California.

Around twenty years ago, someone suggested that he needed to work for a company so that he could qualify for retirement benefits. He came to Austin, Texas, and for two decades worked as a painter.

A small man, his features revealed a pure Indian face. His eyes seemed to be hiding deep within his head, for his protruding high cheekbones so dominated an almost wrinkle-free face. Although he walked on an artificial leg, he appeared in excellent health at the age of 104. His body was of a much younger man. I'd love to have his hearing.

The social worker explained that he was not eligible for a government-supported rest home or nursing home, for he was basically healthy. She said he receives a government income of $401 a month. Representatives from several agencies visit him from time to time ... to check on him ... but also to visit with him, for he is good company. Otherwise, she said, he lives completely alone.

He had a project. It was sitting on a card table by the window. A book, a pad, and a pencil. At 104 years of age, he was teaching himself how to read and write.

TWENTY-FIVE

The Putting Preacher

was an innocent Presbyterian. I never dreamed that there were Baptist preachers lurking out there in Christendom waiting for an opportunity to lure you into Baptisthood. I valued the friendship with this Baptist preacher because he had been recommended to me by the Baptist preacher he replaced as a man I would enjoy knowing and having as a friend. And I had enjoyed his friendship. He was different. He didn't try to sell you his religious beliefs. He didn't meddle with yours. He told good jokes . . . some of them almost clean. He was a former football jock. He has a passion for fishing and especially hunting. He supported his family while enrolled in seminary by killing alligators and selling their hides. His sermons were pure commonsense delight. So I felt secure being friends with the Reverend Dr. Gerald Mann.

During all our good times together, I was being set up. Subtly, cleverly. He lured me to the golf courses. He even occasionally allowed me to beat him in a round of golf. All the time

The Reverend Dr. Gerald Mann. Courtesy Dr. Gerald Mann.

telling funny stories, asking about my welfare, and being a jolly good fellow. Then he zapped me. He did it with a putter.

For seventeen holes, he could have been out-putted by Ray Charles. He would have had to improve to even three putt. And he wailed . . . and ranted . . . and profaned the putting greens and the ball makers and the club makers and the originators of the game of golf. So, on the last hole when he had a forty-five-foot downhill, uphill, undulating putt for a par that would have intimidated our fellow church member Tom Kite, I felt safe in declaring, "Preacher, if you sink that putt, I'll join your church."

Looking heavenward . . . and seemingly about to cross himself, he said, "Done." He lined up . . . looked upward for help once more . . . struck the ball and forty-five feet later heard that beautiful noise that every golfer dreams of as the ball hit the bottom of the cup. He turned with a smirk that was pure-dee Baptist, "Gotcha!"

I said, "The reason I need to join your church is because I'm such a damn liar."

Preacher Mann had been struggling with a new church that for some time held services in a school cafeteria. Now he was building a new church. A year after that dastardly putt, he called me. "Meet me on the number seven green at Hills of Lakeway. We're going to film my incredible putt."

There before a film crew, we re-created the scene. Forty-five feet to the hole . . . I repeated my line, "Preacher, if you sink that putt, I'll join your church" . . . and again he struck the ball which ran through cameraman Gary Pickle's legs as he filmed the route of it all the way into the cup. First take!

The next scene is a close-up of the preacher in the pulpit. Following the sinking of the putt, he says, "At Riverbend Baptist Church, we'll take 'em any way we can get 'em." The camera then pans to me in the front pew nodding assent.

It ran on television as a half-minute commercial. It was applauded by everyone happy to discover a preacher with a sense of humor and was lambasted by every fundamentalist Baptist preacher within three thousand miles of the Southern Baptist Convention.

The ad was highlighted by *USA Today*, received a two-page spread in *Advertising World Magazine*, and was shown on NBC news. Because I believe in truth in advertising, I joined Dr. Mann's church. And thousands have followed. Gerald Mann is now a national television personality and a best-selling author.

Recently I ran into my good friend Monsignor Richard McCabe. He said, "If I knew you were thinking of switching churches, I would have lured you into the Catholic Church."

I replied, "No way, Father. You're a lousy putter."

TWENTY-SIX

Winter Beach

t was a winter beach. Beaches are seasonal, too, like trees.

It was an alive beach. The new norther had exploded a stampede of cold air. The whiter sand of the Mustang Island dunes flew lowly over the darker beach sand like a nervous shroud, almost foglike. The sea oats were bowing in submission. The surf, incredibly, had flattened out in the wind. It was literally blowing the waves down, making them struggle to come into the shore against the norther's cold breath. The crests of the waves were streaming upward and outward like witch's hair.

But on the horizon where the wind had full sweep, the waves looked like huge ruffles. Twelve-footers were keeping the boats in port. Sand was peppering our faces and seeking entry into our squinting eyes.

The willet sandpipers and gulls seemed baffled by the new cold and power of the wind. Birds that were usually territorial were sharing the same area, huddled together like sheep. Two orange-billed black skimmers that you often see flying inches above the water like torpedo divers were wandering aimlessly around the beach, confused. Flights of wild mallards riding with the wind gusts looked like jets swooping to the attack. The cormorants were puzzled, "Why did we decide to come south for the winter?"

The beach belonged to Peg and me and the birds. As far as we could see in any direction . . . to the north toward Port Aransas . . . to the south toward Mexico, nada. Not another soul dared the storm. But we were dressed for it. Sweaters covered with rain suits. Come on . . . have at us! We're ready for you.

But then over the roar of the wind came a new sound. Like raindrops on a tin roof. Incredibly, it was sleet pellets bouncing off our water resistant hoods. Somebody tell the weatherman . . . you don't have sleet on the Texas Coast in October . . . and Halloween wasn't until the next day.

Afterward, the first fire in a new fireplace . . . hot chocolate . . . and a warming smugness knowing that we alone had shared the storm on the beach and were now secure in our cave.

The next morning, another bonus. Warming sunshine. The wind now exhausted . . . the water now blue and asleep. And as we strolled the beach, we harvested our reward for yesterday's adventure. Where the waves lapped the sand, they left hundreds and hundreds of sand dollars. We were rich! And we were enriched.

TWENTY-SEVEN

D-Day Fifty Years After

hey came back. Back to Normandy. Back to the most memorable experience of their lives. Wearing their VFW and American Legion caps, they came back. Once again they were embraced by the French. The supposedly haute French poured out their hearts to these men who had rescued them fifty years before and now have come back to D-Day.

Men who were raised never to show their emotions . . . "Men don't cry, son" . . . still dutifully fighting back the tears, usually unsuccessfully. Tears for the buddies whose graves they have discovered. But also tears of joy for being back to their historical place and time. "I brought Martha to show her where I fought. This is where I came ashore, Martha. And right there is where Sam fell. And then we ran up to this cliff where they couldn't get at us. We weren't heroes. We were just doing the job we were supposed to do, and we were scared to death."

But they were heroes. Still are, and the world so reminded them this fiftieth anniversary.

How wonderful. Men who have reached the age where so often they are greeted with eyes rolling back when they say, "Did I tell you about that time during World War II?" . . . But now the eyes are filled with excitement as the veterans tell their stories. Now the networks, the newspapers, the magazines want to hear their stories. Want them to relive their shining moment.

Good Morning, America on a Sunday morning. I felt for the young interviewer. She had two veterans as her guests. She asked them to share their experiences. But she was asking them to share fifty years in three minutes. How do you condense Hell to a sound bite? As they told their tales, she was more nervous than they had been at the landing, for she could see the clock. They could see only the sands of time.

And how about the audacity of the old guys jumping out of airplanes and parachuting back to the ground where they had landed a half century ago? "For land's sake, Edgar, jumping out of an airplane at your age!"

"Aw, Agnes, it was nothing. It was a piece of cake."

"Well, Edgar, I hope it's soft cake. 'Cause after that jump, your upper plate is missing in action somewhere in Normandy."

At an age when the professional world says it's time for you to step down and make way, they stepped back, for awhile at least, into the spotlight. The Free World applauded them . . . remembered them . . . revered them. The queen came . . . the presidents came . . . the prime ministers came . . . the media came as the veterans came back to Normandy. And we all remembered the word gallantry.

For many it took fifty years of reflection to realize what they had done. Many had to break through the barrier of not wanting to remember, in order to remember. And one of them said, "We are here as old men visiting the graves of our buddies who are lying there as young men. They are forever young. They did not have the chance to reach our age, to experience the life that we have, or to return to this sacred soil and consider what we did . . . who we were . . . and live the consequences of our days on Normandy."

It was like a dream . . . déjà vu.

"Who was that young man to whom this happened? My God! That young man was me."

TWENTY-EIGHT

Eulogy to John

ike most Texans I can't remember when I didn't know John Connally. I do know that I knew Nellie Connally first when she was Idanell Brill. She was my sister Mary Alice's close friend. They were schoolmates in Austin, Texas. For years they alternated titles won . . . Miss Austin, Queen of Austin High School, Class Favorite, etc. Later my first year in radio coincided with Nellie Connally's first year as a salesperson for radio station KTBC in Austin, owned by Lady Bird Johnson.

Perhaps I first saw John Connally on stage. He performed as an actor in University of Texas productions while studying there. He also was president of the student body. Everyone on campus knew John Connally and knew he was going to be a motion picture star or president of, at least, the United States.

I became acquainted with Connally on a personal basis when he fired me from my job as an announcer at KTBC. That'll form a relationship real quick. He had just returned from naval

With John and Nellie Connally and newsman Frank Blair.
Zintgraff Photographers.

duty in the war in the Pacific. Connally and a group of veterans, including his former college roommate Jake Pickle, had applied to the FCC for their own radio station to be called KVET. As one of Lyndon Johnson's "boys," Connally was magnanimously invited to train for his future profession by serving as temporary manager of Lady Bird's radio station. Jake Pickle was cutting his radio eyeteeth by selling advertising for KTBC.

Sensing an opportunity, I immediately applied for a raise in salary that Connally immediately turned down. A conservative in the making. On my next station break, I offered up the following ill-conceived identification: "This is KTBC, the starvation station of the nation." That'll show him, by gawd. I felt as smug as an armadillo that had learned how to kill cars . . . for about twenty seconds.

"Mr. Pryor, report to the manager's office immediately."

Even before I was fully into the room, I was blasted with, "You're fired!"

"But why?"

"For that station break you just made."

"But you can't fire me."

"Why can't I?"

"Because you don't know anything about radio." (I'd been in it for three weeks at the time.)

Connally leaned back in his chair, his hands behind his head, stared at the ceiling, and broke out into that beautiful, loud laugh that served him so well throughout his life and said, "Well, I 'spect that's true. But don't do it again."

Throughout the years, I watched Connally's incredible life unfold. Our paths crossed many times, many ways. Though not of the same political cut, I liked the man. I respected his courage, his talent, his sense of humor. And when he died, I shared these words with my radio audience:

He was beautiful.
He was ambitious.
He was smart.
He was tough as the boots he often wore.
He was shrewd.
He was a Hollywood star without a picture.
He was a president without a presidency.
He was a millionaire without the millions.
He was a Texas ring-tailed-tooter, and for seventy-six years he
    blew through this country like a Texas blue norther. And
    you knew he was here. He made a difference.
Big John. Big John Connally.
You can't help it. You can't help but miss him. You can't help but
    miss him whether a Democrat, Republican, Perot-ite, rich
    man, poor man, black man, white man, red man, brown
    man, old man, young man, or woman.
He was part of Texas.
A big part of Texas who became a big part of this nation.

He was a big part of Lyndon Johnson. He was there at the beginning in Washington, D.C. He was there when it was time for someone to tell LBJ it was time for him to leave D.C. And he always had the guts to tell LBJ what he thought LBJ should hear.

He was a big part of The University of Texas. President of the student body. Married its sweetheart. Starred on its stages. Earned his education there and used it in so many ways. He never left the University he so loved.

He was part of the good war. He stood his ground on a scarred and bloody deck as the Japanese kamikazes hurled themselves at him off the ragged and raw shores of Okinawa. And he became Secretary of that Navy.

Three times he was our governor. Three times he was a good one.

He made education better. He made us smarter. He had the audacity to believe that people outside the Red River and the Rio Grande could be enticed to vacation in Texas . . . in hot, dusty, wild, and woolly Texas. And now they come by the thousands and bring their money to Texas.

He caught an assassin's bullet that blasted its way through his body. He survived the attack that his friend John F. Kennedy didn't.

He became Secretary of the Treasury. And he wanted more. He wanted to do more for his country.

A lifelong Democrat, he had the bodaciousness to switch . . . to change.

And when he failed in the big step, just as when he sat with his wife before the nation and watched the auctioneers sell the trappings of their lives . . . he had the guts to smile . . . and then pick himself up and start all over again.

Like a rodeo rider brushing the dust off his jeans and climbing back into the saddle.

He should have been a movie star.

He should have been at the Alamo.

He should have been president.

He should have lived years more.

He should not have done a lot of things he did.

But because he did so many things he should have done and because he was a ring-tailed-tooter who blew through Texas like a blue norther, Big John left some big, wonderful tracks.

Big John.

Big Bad John.

Big Good John.

And now, good-bye, John.

TWENTY-NINE

The Leper

 asked myself, "Why are we here? Why are Peggy and I on mules riding down one of the world's highest sea cliffs on mules on a trail not much wider than the twenty-dollar bill we paid for the privilege?"

It had seemed a good day for the journey. We had stood on top of the rain forest mountain that looks down on the incredibly beautiful Kalaupapa Peninsula of the Hawaiian island of Molokai. The stretch of land created by the small volcano Kauhako appeared as a green leaf almost two thousand feet below. The buildings on Kalaupapa looked like doll-houses and from that distance as innocent. The Pacific stretched out forever to the north and to the visible Maui to the east, assuring us that there were other lands in this world. I had long wanted to visit the last remaining leper colony on the Islands and to tape some interviews for my radio show. So when we read that people could visit the site of the colony on mule back, we chose to go. And that, Richard, is why we are riding down the historic, narrow Pali Trail, trusting our lives to four-footed animals.

We were joined by other tourists. None of them appeared foolish adventurers. True, most of them appeared much younger than I but, then, so are most people I encounter nowadays. We had guides, and the price was right. I kept waiting for Peggy to tell me she'd rather not go, and she kept waiting to hear the same words from me. A chicken standoff. So there.

The words "switch" and "back" had never been pleasant ones to me. I associated them with where mother applied the peach tree switches when she deemed it necessary to correct my misdeeds. I was soon to learn that the two words joined as in "switchback" were even more ominous. In Molokai a switchback is a turn in the trail. A trail that winds down a sheer cliff. A trail from which scores of people, cows, horses, even goats have fallen to their nevermore. The Pali Trail, the only thin strand of possible escape for the lepers of yore, who were brought in boats and dumped on the Kalaupapa Peninsula beginning in the year 1865 by decree of King Kamehameha V. The more advanced cases were to be sent to the island of Molokai, where a leprosy settlement was established at Kalawao on the Kalaupapa Peninsula. There to fend for themselves.

In descending the trail, you must negotiate these switchbacks. Well, actually you don't have to negotiate them, but the alternative is less than desirable or survivable. When my mule came to the first switchback, he stopped as if considering, as if contemplating . . . what? His demise? I didn't dare even to think of influencing his movement. Then he started shuffling his feet on the slippery rock trail. My God! (Did I hear a yes?) The animal is going to go forward. As he made the turn, my body was extended for a moment over an abyss that was nothing but hundreds of feet of nothing. And at the bottom was something! Rocks . . . craggy volcanic, body-ripping rocks. Actually the mule had to contort its body into an S-shape in order to make the turn.

It was worse for Peggy than for me. She was on the mule behind me. She had to watch it happen, realizing that whatever happened to me would probably happen to her. Macho man, I whistled a tune as I went around the worst fright since my first algebra book. Peg said, "If you're going to whistle, try something besides 'Nearer My God to Thee.'"

We made the first turn, breathed a mega sigh of relief only to hear the jolly words, "Well, that's number one. Only twenty-five more to go."

As we got close enough to the bottom to hear the roar of the waves hitting the rocks, we felt more secure making the switchbacks. Now only a three-hundred-foot fall.

The beauty of the scene unfolding replaced our fear. The little village of the lepers below became more than rooftops. It took on bright, happy colors. The lush vegetation entered our senses with its fragrances and visual feasts.

Soon we could see the bus waiting for us at the bottom, obviously brought in by boat years before. When we reached the comfort of flat land, there awaited our school bus. Wait'll I tell my grandchildren this one. "When I was a student I rode a mule two thousand feet down a cliff to school." The driver of the bus was also our teacher and our guide. He was Richard Marks, a leper.

We were at his home, the leper settlement on Kalaupapa. He is a moderately tall man with a mischievous gleam in his left eye. His right eye had been a victim of Hansen's disease, leprosy. His voice was not the musical, soft voice you expect from the Islanders who live so close to nature. His delivery was staccato . . . his accent more Brooklyn than Molokai . . . his sentences laced with well-chosen mild profanities. I asked him if I might tape his comments as he drove us along over the semiroads.

"No problem. I'm the local historian here. Lately the publicity we have gotten has brought TV and movie producers from all over the world."

He turned the ignition key, the motor resisted . . . then coughed . . . then grudgingly began its work. Marks gave us a running commentary as we drove through the small village. As I glanced out my window, I saw a nun in a black habit down to her ankles walking on water!

"Well, I see that Sister Marie's out fishing again. Whenever she gets an hour break, she grabs her rod and reel and stands out there on the rocks in that old habit, fishing. Every now and then, a wave'll come along and wash her off. She just climbs back on and keeps on fishing. She's seventy-four years old."

Sitting by Marks was his dog that would exit at every stop and then somehow manage to be sitting in his regular place just as the bus pulled out again.

Marks continued, "Now you probably won't see any of the lepers. There are eighty-six of them remaining on the peninsula. Most of them are pretty well up in age. They have chosen to live here. The sulfone drug that arrests the spread of leprosy now allows lepers to live pretty much where they want to. These people are happy here. But this time of day, they're in watching the soap operas, viewing the tragedies of an urban existence."

We did see a few lepers in the small airport terminal alongside the landing strip. They wore sunglasses, as the disease makes sunlight somewhat painful. Noticeable were the stubs of what had been fingers. It was also interesting to note that the somewhat deformed faces all seemed to be wearing smiles.

Our tour continued. "Now there's one of our churches, and there's the school, and over here you'll see our medical clinic. We used to have a hospital, but it burned down. Over there used to be what we called our patient building. It was where patients could be visited by relatives. There was barbed wire all around it. The patients went in the right door, and the visitors went in the left door. There was a double wall between them and a quarter-inch wire fence separated them. We had to go through all this long after they gave up that damn nonsense in the continental United States. The Hawaiian Board of Health controls this county. They wanted to keep reminding us that we were lepers. They wanted to make damn sure we never forgot it. This protected a lot of jobs in the Board of Health. Too often they had some turkey in charge who found it too much trouble to read something new. So they kept the old laws in force here until the news of the new ways became too public to ignore. That was in 1968. We've got a good Board of Health now with a real doctor instead of a politician running it."

As we drove by a cemetery, I noticed a bungalow sitting right in the middle of the graves. "What's that about, Richard?"

"Well, the man who built that house put it there as a matter of convenience. He had three wives and eleven of his thirteen children buried there. He didn't have leprosy, but all three wives died of illnesses brought about by the disease. The children weren't lepers. They died of diphtheria and whooping cough. Stuff like that, which the visitors brought to the Islands. Between 1830 and 1885, two out of three of the pure Hawaiians died by the age of thirty-six."

I asked him how he first came to the Kalaupapa settlement.

"My father was diagnosed as having leprosy. I was just a kid. I lost my grandmother, father, uncle, and cousin to the effects of leprosy. It's like AIDS in that respect. No one dies of it . . . it just lowers your resistance until something else gets you. AIDS is the new leprosy. I travel around making talks about that now. I don't want to see happen to them what happened to me . . . when they came to school and rounded us up . . . embarrassed us in front of our playmates. Our neighbors wouldn't let their kids play with us. They warned my nine-year-old classmate to keep an eye on me because I had leprosy in my family. And if I got a blister or red mark, turn me in because they knew I wouldn't turn myself in. 'If you don't, he might give leprosy to you.' You know, no matter how you feel about AIDS, they're human beings. You don't kick 'em. If you don't like 'em, stay the hell away from them . . . but don't kick 'em when they're down. Fear is needed . . . but common sense is needed with the fear."

By this time, we were driving down toward the end of the peninsula. The valley was verdant, lush tropical growth everywhere. The eternal blue to our left was one with the blue above. To the right, always the top lands.

There was almost a collective gasp of delight as we arrived

at the site of our picnic lunch. The trail that we had followed brought us to where a small inlet ends the sliver of lava that is Kalaupapa. The indentation into land is dotted with a small hunk of an island, perhaps once a part of the imprisoning three-thousand-foot sea cliffs above.

Here sitting in deep, green grass under a wanderlusting banyan tree, we enjoyed our lunch. The irony. We had come to one of the most beautiful spots in the Hawaiian Islands that for over eight thousand lepers was once hell on Earth.

After our lunch, I sat with Richard Marks on a stone wall overlooking the ocean. I asked him to tell me of this beautiful and scarred plot of earth.

"In 1865 An Act to Prevent the Spread of Leprosy was signed into law by King Kamehameha V. This act authorized the setting apart of land for isolating persons with leprosy. The Kalihi Hospital was opened near Honolulu for milder or just suspected cases. The more severe cases were sent to the settlement on Molokai. Right out there in that inlet, ships would come and literally dump the victims into the sea. They gave them ten days of food. They were supposed to be able to live off the land and the sea. There were some wooden shacks for shelter. However, the taro roots from which poi is made must be cooked. There was no wood with which to cook the roots nor to repair the shelters. Wild goats had eaten most of the vegetation. The stronger of the lepers took over the place. They formed bands. When the newcomers arrived, they would grab them and take all their food, clothing, and other possessions. They would kidnap the women and force them into prostitution. When missionaries would arrive, they were greeted with the gang's little trick. They would take the worst-case leper on the peninsula, strip him of his clothes, strip a new arrival of his clothes, and then rub the leper all over him. Whereupon the missionary would immediately swim back to the boat that had brought him.

"In 1872 a thirty-three-year-old Catholic priest from Belgium, Father Damien, came ashore here, and the toughs gave him their same little trick. But he was tougher than they were.

He knocked a few heads together and started organizing and civilizing the settlement. He was an expert carpenter. He built houses, churches, a hospital. He planted orchards, brought in cattle, piped in water. Twelve years later, he was diagnosed as having leprosy. Four years later, he died on this peninsula. But Father Damien with the work he did here focused the world's attention on the plight of the lepers. Well, time to be getting along. Everyone back in the bus."

As we were driving back, I talked to Marks about his own story. "When did you first realize you had leprosy?"

"I was twenty-one years of age. I guess I had gotten it from my dad when I was a kid. Hawaiian law said that if you were living with lepers you had to come in every month for a physical or the cops would come get you. I had gone to Hong Kong to avoid those physicals. Well, I was in a motorcycle accident while there. When I got back on my feet, I noticed the red spots and discoloration of my skin. I knew what it was. So I went back to Molokai. I didn't want to stay there. I knew that was a life sentence. So I got them to send me by navy ship to the leper settlement in Louisiana. I was lucky. The sulfone drug was available then. My disease was brought under control there. From there I went to school in Arizona. They didn't know I was a leper. They didn't want lepers there. So to hide my condition, I went to California each month to buy my medicine. Otherwise, the Arizona officials would have shipped me back to Louisiana. But then Arizona began checking the pharmacies in California. So I moved on to Chicago and school for a couple of years. Same thing happened there. I finished a couple of courses and moved to Santa Monica. I had another motorcycle wreck there. With my resistance lowered, I could feel the disease coming on again. So back to Molokai. I was going to stay for about a year. My dad was losing his sight."

"Richard," I asked, "what went on in your mind when you first learned that you had leprosy?"

As he searched his mind, his foot inadvertently, I suppose, came down harder on the accelerator. "It drove me up the wall.

I'd seen it happen to so many members of my family. I knew it was a life sentence. I knew there was medicine, but it was still unpredictable. My grandmother and uncle went totally blind. My Dad lost his right eye as did I from the medication. But what can you do? There are worse things. We're finding that out now. And I had my sense of humor. You laugh or you die."

I asked, "Where are you now in your life and your health?"

"I'm working twice as hard as I've ever worked before. Feeling better than I have in forty-five years. I've got a good wife and two healthy boys and three healthy girls. I have to be careful. The disease attacks the surface nerves. I can't drink coffee for fear of burning my throat without feeling it. Sometimes I'll be working on a motor or something hot and smell something burning, and it's me. I'm making talks all around. I went to India in 1984. I was the first leper invited to the International Leprosy Conference. I got to meet Mother Teresa. Someone introduced me to her and said that I was a leper from Molokai. She said, 'Yes, I can see that.' Then she nudged me in the ribs and said, 'I bet you know Father Damien.' I said, 'Sister, I'm not that old. He died over one hundred years ago.' She said, 'He was my hero. When I was about five years old, my mother read a history of Damien to me. Then when I was about nine years old in school, I read another book about Damien. That's when I decided to be a missionary and work with lepers in foreign places.' Then she kissed me on the cheek.

"I see Sister Marie is still fishing. It must be good today.

"Well, folks, here's where you get out and get on. I used to own part of the mule rides, but I got out. Too many accidents."

With those ominous words ringing in our ears, we headed up toward the top lands, up the Pali Trail from Kalaupapa.

THIRTY

Song-and-Dance Man

unday is Father's Day. I re-
member, especially, that Daddy was a song-and-dance man. He
toured the vaudeville circuits of this nation. Like Al Jolson and
Eddie Cantor, "Skinny" Pryor did a black-face act back when it
was considered acceptable for a white man to portray a black man.

Dad married Mother fairly late in his life. When one trav-
els the land with a chorus line, marriage is not the first thought.
But he wore his voice out. No microphones then to amplify.
Shout it out! Sing it fortissimo. "Mammy, Mammy. I'd walk a
thousand miles for one of your smiles, my Mammy."

The baritone became a rasp, and Dad got off the road. Came
back to Austin, Texas, to stay in show business as the operator of
a second-run motion picture theater. He named it the Grand
Central, but everyone called it Skinny's, for he was the theater.
More of an attraction on the outside of the theater than Buck
Jones, Hoot Gibson, and Ken Maynard inside the theater. For
Dad brought his showmanship to Congress Avenue. Always

out in front either selling tickets or hawking 'em in. Wearing a black beret, a straw boater, or a derby to cover his bald head, he'd use his vaudeville days persona to lure customers, even if they didn't have the fifteen cents for adults or the nickel for the kids' admission. Eggs, chickens, or vegetables were often the price of admission.

He missed the stage . . . the applause . . . the affirmation that all entertainers seek. So every now and then, Dad would do his old routines for the good people of Austin, Texas.

I vividly remember those initial impressions that became indelibly part of me. Dad sitting at the piano at home singing "Yes, we have no bananas, we have no bananas today." And "When you are cold and on the street, who says here's two-bits, go and eat? Nobody." Theme songs of the Depression years.

Strange that I remember as if yesterday the first performance by Dad that I ever witnessed. It was at Baker School, where mother was president of the PTA for a record number of years. "The Pryors just keep 'em coming." I was in kindergarten at Baker. It was an evening of variety acts for some school cause. Dad was the star of the night. He did his old sand dance. Sprinkled sand from my sandpile on the floor and with his dancing feet made all kinds of remarkable sounds, including the musical noise of a train slowly taking off and then gaining speed until it was roaring down the track. He made you see it. He sang a few songs with his now gravelly voice. Then he told a joke. And with the telling of that joke, somewhere in the labyrinth of the ventricles, glands, cor- puscles of that little five-year-old boy's mind, and perhaps soul, something clicked, and I said, "Yeah. That's what I want to do. I want to make people laugh and be happy."

I don't remember jokes. I make them up. But I remember the joke that Dad told that arrested me for life. It was about Mrs. Hall, a geography teacher at Baker. She was a large woman, obviously fond of eating. And Dad said, "I was talking to Mrs. Hall. She told me she would give half her life for a watermelon. So I went out and bought her two." And there was laughter . . . beautiful, addicting laughter. I am forever amazed that I was

"Skinny" Pryor, song-and-dance man.

so impressed with that silly little gag that it has never left me. Also, impressed that I got the point. I've never been good in arithmetic.

And so the die was cast. That would be it. Dad introduced me to the world of entertainment, and I shall always be there.

Like the songs he sang, Dad had gay songs and sad songs in his life. His sad song came in a bottle that would never empty. In a way, Dad became the town drunk . . . but in a town that loved him, that nurtured him, that protected him. "Saw Skinny standing out in front of Seton Hospital last night wrapped in a sheet. I figured Dr. Goddard had checked him in there to sober him up again and hid his clothes. So I gave him a ride home in my taxi."

We kids often lived the lyrics of one of the songs Dad used to sing, "Father, dear father, come home with me now." One of my first life memories is going into a saloon with mother to try to persuade Dad to come home. And he did come home sober most of the time and sometimes even happy. But when Dad went on one of his drinking sprees, the whole town knew it. And Dallas as well. "Mr. Skinny had a drinking problem. But he's a nice man. He lets me in his movie just for going after a glass of water for him. He drinks a lot. But he's a nice man."

And when he sobered up, he was sorry for where he'd been. He'd sit in the living room, looking at the floor, rubbing his bald head while listening to Edward R. Murrow on the radio. I figured lots of times, Dad wasn't there. He was on the stage in some far-off town, doing his dance, singing his songs with a clear, loud voice, and listening to the applause.

I never learned to dance. Two left feet in two right shoes. I tried. My old buddy who danced and joked on Broadway, Leo Herzog, tried valiantly to teach me to tap dance. He was giving voice lessons to a rock.

But the other night, Dad came back to me. It was in a large dance hall. The walls were lined with people. And Dad took me in his arms, and we danced together. He was wearing his familiar black suit with a white shirt and a black bow tie. I felt the softness of that suit. There was the pleasant smell of a rose in his lapel, and there was no odor of alcohol. And we floated over that dance floor. It was like dancing on a cloud. Dad was magnificent as he led me in all kind of wonderful steps with swoops and spins and dips and slides. We danced as one as the enthralled audience watched in amazement and delight, not at all surprised to see a boy dancing with his father. When we finished, the applause seemed to be forever. And it is.

THIRTY-ONE

The Love Couple

orty years they had been married. "The perfect couple" they were called by everyone who knew them. Compatible in every way. She, a nest-maker.

Their home was a paragon of domesticity. And within that house, everywhere you turned, there were evidences of her affection for her husband. Little needlepoint slogans framed on the walls with words like, "I love my husband"; "Home is when my husband is here"; "Love me, love my husband." Constant love notes. Almost any hour of the day, you could smell her love for him. The fragrance of a roast cooking or bread baking. There was no doubting this woman's love for her husband.

Nor his for her. The lawn displayed it. Frequently he would let the grass grow high then cut out her name with the lawnmower, surrounded by a heart. He planted yellow roses, her favorite flower, in a heart-shaped flowerbed by the steps. He handmade their mailbox, and the name on it read: Mr. and Mrs. Leonard Smertz . . . Love Couple.

The boat that he parked in the driveway was named *Love Boat*. They were voted the most loving couple by their church. They frequently appeared on talk shows to discuss the techniques for maintaining a happy marriage. They were named Mr. and Mrs. Love Bug of South Junction two years straight during the annual Bag Worm Festival. Yes, they were the perfect couple.

Then one day, like a bolt out of the blue that always seemed to hover over their home, it happened. He walked into their home and said to her, "Sorry, dear, but you'll have to leave. Our marriage is over."

Five minutes later, after he revived her from a world-class swoon, she gasped, "Leave? Our marriage over? But why?"

"It's very simple, my dearest. It has been decreed by the U.S. Fish and Wildlife Service. Our yard has become a habitat for the purple-tongued finch and pigeon-toed woodpeckers. And a Sicilian bag beetle has taken up residence in the cellar. The Fish and Wildlife Service says that there's not enough room for them and both of us, so you have to go."

"But why me? Why not you?" she queried with concerned query.

"Because they have informed me that I have to maintain and protect their habitat," he responded to her concerned query. "And since I do the yard work and repair work, you get the short straw."

"Yes . . . I can see the logic of that, having once been a government employee myself," she said sobbingly. "Is there . . . is there any chance we might come together again . . . in this life, I mean?"

"There is one chance," her husband responded arithmetically. "If you could possibly manage to have yourself declared an endangered species, we just might pull it off."

"Yes," she replied concurringly, "perhaps we could do that. Maybe I could become classified as a savings and loan executive."

They embraced, kissed, and she walked out the door . . . past the yellow roses . . . past the *Love Boat* . . . past her name, Thelma, standing tall in green grass letters, surrounded by a heart, in front of their loving home.

THIRTY-TWO

The Duke of Wayne

very year the experience becomes more and more incredible. As the legend of John Wayne continues to grow, to have a life of its own, more and more I realize the great fortune that allowed me to experience him close up and live. It's happened to me all my life . . . to walk blindly into the shadows of greatness without seeking it.

I chose to live where I was born, in Austin, Texas. Yet many times, I've been privileged to say those heady words, "Ladies and gentlemen, the president of the United States." As a lifelong member of Lady Bird Johnson's broadcast companies, I also served as Lyndon Johnson's "favorite emcee" and sometimes court jester. I was privileged to entertain and meet two chancellors of Germany, two presidents of Mexico, the president of Pakistan, and numerous ambassadors and other political figures.

As a master of ceremonies with a penchant for roasting, I shared the rostrum with former Presidents Reagan, Ford, Carter, and Bush.

As an after-dinner speaker, I was invited numerous times by Speaker Jim Wright to address members of Congress. As a television interviewer, I had ten grand years as co-host of a weekly television show with the legendary University of Texas football coach Darrell Royal, traveling with him and the team during the glory years of wishbone and national championships. Also, I had a centennial-year season of U.T. football in the same role with the current University of Texas coach, John Mackovic.

During the years when Hollywood stars often ventured out into the hinterlands with their films, I became their on-stage interviewer. I had the rare opportunity to become acquainted and work and sometimes travel with such stars as James Stewart, Raquel Welch, Lucille Ball, Charleton Heston, Gregory Peck, James Arness, Fred McMurray, Joan Crawford, George Peppard, Dean Martin, Dan Blocker, Danny Thomas, Carol Channing, Helen Hayes, and Bob Hope. This is blatant name-dropping, but I'm still amazed that I experienced these names to drop. As one who chose middle-sized Austin, Texas, as my arena for a radio and TV career, I achieved swiftly fleeting glory by reflection. It added very little to the family coffers, but it made one helluva fine scrapbook.

Now, years later, as I look back on that scrapbook and turn to the page that bears the world famous face of John Wayne, I realize, "By gawd! I got to know that man."

It was the world premier of his movie *War Wagon* in Dallas. Interstate Theaters hired me as emcee to interview him during his stage appearances in Dallas and Fort Worth. They also asked me to be master of ceremonies for a sixty-fifth birthday party for the Duke at Six Flags over Texas.

I used up my lifelong supply of courage and chose to roast the mighty man. With palpitating heart and shaky hands, I threw barb after barb. Lifesavingly, he enjoyed it. He roared with laughter, and I overheard him say to his son Michael, "We gotta get this guy in one of our movies." His word was as good as his Scotch. Several months later, I received a personal call from

Wayne inviting me for a small role in *Green Berets* and later in *Hellfighters*. I said, "I don't have an agent."

He replied, "You've got one now. Me."

While on the set of *Berets* at Fort Benning, Georgia, he would frequently ask me to write a funny line for a scene. I also wrote at his request a speech that he delivered to an audience of military brass. Later he asked me to rework the screenplay of his film in which he depicted firefighter Red Adair, *Hell Fighters*. He didn't like the Hollywood dialogue. He wanted more Texas reality in language and oil field attitudes. The screenwriters guild would not allow my work, since I was not a member of their union. However, for the rest of my life, I have been able to display the check John Wayne paid me to write him a script.

Ever since the trip to the mountaintop, I have been asked by scores and scores of Wayne worshipers, "What was John Wayne really like?" And I suppose all of the hordes of us who came even close to Wayne answer that with great authority. Much like the critics of Edna Ferber's *Giant* who claimed she researched her book by flying low over Texas in a very fast airplane.

But I did have the rare chance to see him close-up on quite a few occasions. He directed *Green Berets*, and I saw Wayne the director at work for six weeks. I saw a man amazingly similar to another giant I knew, Lyndon Johnson. I'm not talking politics. I'm talking personality, character. There was a physical similarity. Both Wayne and Johnson, a John Wayne movie fan, incidentally, confirmed the number of times their comparable physical characteristics had been pointed out to them. Physical men. Taller in life than on screen. Both dominated by sheer height, and they knew how to use it. Both as direct as a .30-.30 Winchester at close range. The famous temper of LBJ would narrow his eyes to slits like the slots in a tank through which the machine guns were fired. Wayne's eyes became almost Oriental, nearly shut to avoid the fire coming from his nostrils. They both were explosive and had no need to muffle the explosion. They shared it with whomever. And yet, once delivered, their wrath, like the smoke and sound of an exploded bomb, floated

John "Duke" Wayne and "friendly Indians." Frances Photographers.

further and further away in a breeze that you wished was faster. And then, almost always, a gesture of some kind, usually not direct, that reminded the wounded that they were still friends. There was tenderness inside that toughness.

Loyalty was an important trait for John Wayne, as it was for Lyndon Johnson. The lists of casts for Wayne's movies tell the story. Look them up. Notice the repetition in names, not only among the featured players but in such categories as stuntmen, travel directors, makeup men and women. You see many of the same faces in numerous Wayne movies. His son Michael was often the producer and ran Wayne's Batjac Production. His son Patrick often had an acting role, as he did in *Green Berets*. Johnson considered loyalty the eleventh commandment. Thou shalt be loyal to thy leader. And thy leader shalt be loyal to thee . . . sometimes even to a fault. The Texas accents that surrounded President Johnson attested to his passion for loyalty.

Both Cutty Sark men, Wayne and LBJ. Both chili eaters. Wayne insisted that there be a large container of hot chili on the set of *Green Berets* every morning. You had to be brave to partake. You had to be braver not to. It was expected. But Wayne's chili would have bothered LBJ. Real Texans don't cotton to beans in their chili.

A vast political gulf existed between Wayne and LBJ. Though once more conservative, by the time of his presidency Lyndon Johnson had become much more progressive. Duke Wayne was notoriously conservative, though he would fool you at times with his opinions. I'm told he favored the deliverance of the Panama Canal back into the hands of the Panamanians. Certainly, there was no argument between the two men regarding the decision to stand up against communism in Vietnam. *Green Berets* was Wayne's political statement about that war.

Both macho men, Wayne and LBJ. Proud of their manhood. Tough in language. Wayne's eloquence in profanity was almost Shakespearean, as fluent in Spanish as in English. LBJ sometimes ventured a bit past "dadgummit." Johnson treasured his Silver Star for his participation in warfare. Wayne's silver star was a bracelet given to him by the Montagnard native warriors of Vietnam with whom he shared incoming fire while visiting them.

Both men had known serious illnesses. Both men refused to give in to them.

It was at his birthday party at Six Flags that the Duke flaunted his disdain for weakness most dramatically. He was still recovering from the removal of a cancerous lung. It slowed him down only temporarily. His speech was more breathy, and his walk was not as fast. But otherwise, he was the very physical John Wayne we see on the screen.

Sitting at the head table that night with Wayne was Raymond Willie, head of Interstate Theaters, the mammoth Dallas-based theater chain. Willie, pale and frail, was only a few days out of the hospital where he had been treated for a life-threatening illness. It required considerable courage and dedication for him to be there. But his respect and fondness for Wayne gave him the strength to attend the birthday banquet. When as toastmaster, I introduced Willie, Wayne shouted out, "Stand up, Raymond! Show them, by god, that you can still stand up!"

Willie clutched the arms of his chair, doggedly strained to lift himself and then stood up to the applause of the large audience.

Friends told me that when Wayne's last bout with cancer had struck and the end was near he resisted pain-killing drugs as much as he could. He wanted to be lucid during his last hours with his family and friends. So to the very last sequence of his life drama, he was the strong, tough man we saw on the screen. The old law officer in *The Shootist*. The cowman in *The Cowboys*, fighting to the death his death. Proud and nonwhimpering to the last breath.

What was John Wayne really like? Like the brave Marine who attacked the Japanese on the sands of Iwo Jima. Like the naval officer who took his submarine through the nets of Tokyo harbor. In many ways, he was the pilot who flew his Marine combat plane into the very face of the kamikazes. He was the man who fought to the death in the Alamo, battled the marauding Indians tooth and nail, and held off the Vietcong as long as possible. That John Wayne really was.

THIRTY-THREE

Ambassador Davis

ecretary of State Dean
Rusk said that James Davis created more international goodwill
with his barbecued ribs than the entire U.S. State Department.
He has cooked for John F. Kennedy, Chancellors Adenauer and
Erhard of Germany, several presidents of Mexico, President
Ayub Kahn of Pakistan, Vice President Hubert Humphrey, and
numerous senators and presidential cabinet members. And all
because he answered an advertisement on an Austin television
station. Lady Bird Johnson's television station.

He was well qualified. He had been a cook in the U.S. Navy
from 1941 to 1945. He literally cooked all over the world as a
member of the merchant marine from 1946 to 1952. The next
three years, he spent as a food service supervisor for the Veterans Hospital in Houston. And from 1955 to 1959, he was the
second cook at a restaurant in Austin. He answered a television
ad seeking a couple to help at a ranch with cooking, gardening,
pool maintenance, and other duties. On September 22, 1959,

James Davis and his wife, Mary, went to work for the Lyndon B. Johnson family.

They didn't know it at the time, but the Johnsons were not only getting an expert for all of those jobs, they were also hiring a great diplomat and a friend who would be with them all of their lives.

For Texans a good meat cook is more important than a good tax accountant. VIPs from throughout the world have clamored for James' cooking secrets after visiting the LBJ Ranch. James says you cook meat by feel. "I can tell when meat is medium rare just by the way it feels to my fingertips. But you can tell by time and temperature, too. Cook tenderloin 450 degrees for thirty minutes, and it will be medium rare."

Some of the world's most famous people have eaten vegetables from the garden James has planted annually for Mrs. Johnson at the LBJ Ranch. "We planted turnip and mustard greens, tomatoes, okra, squash, eggplants ... stuff like that. People were always saying how much they liked the vegetables. Mrs. Johnson would sometimes tell them that they could have some of the vegetables to take home with them if they would pick them themselves. But they usually didn't."

When LBJ became vice president, he brought James along to be their main man at their home, The Elms, in Washington. But it was soon apparent that he was more important to them at the ranch back in Texas. "So after six months, he tells me that he needs me back on the Pedernales to get things back in shape. But I told him I had already bought a trailer house in which to live while working at The Elms. He asked me where I bought it. I told him. I got my money back, and they got their trailer back."

James says that he learned early in his relationship with LBJ that the best way to get along was to get along. "The further I stayed away from him, the better it was. Do the job and stay outta the way. That was the secret. That man could look you in the eye and read your mind (very much like James Davis). He never gave me hell unless I deserved it. But he sure could do a good job of it. He would make you use your brain. He'd tell you what to do, but he wouldn't tell you how to do it. Now Mrs. Johnson, she will get after you too, if you need it. But she always does it in a nice way and with humor."

President Johnson gave the Davis family a calf when their second daughter was born. "The president said he would give me a yearling calf if we would name that boy Lyndon. The boy was a girl, and we named her Lynda. That got us the calf."

One of James' more interesting assignments was to precede the Johnsons on their frequent winter trips to Acapulco. "I would go down early and take all the food and water. I had to do a lot of planning and shopping to make sure we had plenty to eat. Just like the Secret Service had to take along a lot of golf balls. The president liked to golf down there, and it took a lot of golf balls."

LBJ was a lid lifter and a food taster. James said that whenever they were giving a dinner with some VIP guests you could count on him bringing all the guests through the kitchen, introducing them to the kitchen help, and giving them a spoon to taste what was cooking.

"I loved Vice President Humphrey. I cried when he died. He was such a nice man. I liked Secretary of State Dean Rusk, too. He talked to you like you were somebody. We talked about foreign affairs, the economy, and barbecued ribs. Now Secretary of State Henry Kissinger, he talked to me like I was somebody who was there to wait on him. I didn't care too much for him. But I've had a good life. I've flown on Air Force One. I have a John F. Kennedy rocking chair. President Kennedy personally gave me one of his famous PT-boat pens. Chancellor Adenauer of Germany gave me a special cigarette lighter.

"President Johnson was easier to work for when he came back to the ranch after the White House years. We worked side by side mending fences, dipping and branding cattle, laying pipe. And after work, he'd gather all the hands around the barn behind the house, and he'd talk to us about politics and how to handle our money. We'd have a beer or two, and he'd have Scotch and soda."

James Davis came with many talents. One is a juicy sense of humor. It blesses him . . . it has saved him . . . and it endears him. He is a man comfortable with himself and thus with all those he has encountered. He chops well in varied fields of cotton.

James Davis continues to work four hours a day with Mrs. Johnson at her home in the hills overlooking Austin. "We have a pact, Mrs. Johnson and I. She said she would stick with me as long as I live if I would stick with her as long as she lives."

They both got a good deal.

THIRTY-FOUR

The Homeplace

h, I wish I was in the land of cotton. Old times there are not forgotten. Look away . . . look away . . . look away Dixieland."

I had to learn to hate that song and the Confederate flag that symbolized slavery. Learn because I had been carefully taught by my grandmother and aunts that my roots and allegiance belonged to Dixie. Taught that our family home was in the heart of Dixie, in Greenville, South Carolina. Taught that the Confederacy was something of which we Southerners should be proud.

But thank God I also had other teachers, like my father, who was adored by every Hispanic kid who could gain admittance to his second-run cowboy picture show simply by getting him a glass of water. He championed the cause of biracial admittance to Austin, Texas, theaters. And my dear friend John Henry Faulk, whose family offered a haven in our city for all minorities. Gradually I learned. I learned of the continuing imprisoning of a race of people.

Even so, I had a yearning to see the old homeplace. There was always a picture of the Greenville homeplace on Grandmother's wall . . . a brown, faded photograph. A stone house, the front of it almost obscured by trees and bushes. Not very imposing. But my roots were there, and I wanted to see the family birthing place.

One springlike February day recently, I succumbed to that genetic tugging. Peggy and I went to Greenville, South Carolina. A sister-in-law had discovered a distant relative living in Atlanta. She gave her the exciting news that the old family cemetery was still there in a suburb of Greenville . . . behind the house of a professor at Furman University. We contacted his wife, and she kindly offered to be our guide.

Greenville was a much larger city than I expected. I still saw the community through the eyes of Grandmother Pryor. The streets should be dirt and filled with horses and buggies. People should be sitting on front porches strumming banjos, drinking mint juleps in the shade of magnolia trees. Women should be wearing sunbonnets and hoopskirts, and the men should be in frocktail coats. The fields should be full of cotton. We found, instead, modern, mostly brick buildings and the ubiquitous clichés of American appetites . . . McDonald's, Wendy's, Taco Bell, Kentucky Fried Chicken.

On a clear and crisp day in which the crocus had beaten spring to South Carolina, we entered the family cemetery, no larger than our backyard. Historic, sacred earth to me. And there they were . . . two slabs lying side by side. Great-great-grandfather Captain William Young and my great-great-grandmother Mary Young. His inscription, still readable, told us that he enlisted at the age of sixteen in the Continental Army. He rose to the rank of captain. He fought with George Washington in many major battles of the Revolutionary War . . . had been wounded and was a hero. Was known as the "Terror of the Tories."

The other inscription told us that Mary Young was a loving wife and a dedicated member of the Baptist Church. We wandered around the family tree . . . a family reunion. Ancient

The Captain Billy Young House, Greenville, South Carolina.
Photo by Peggy Davis Pryor.

relatives introduced to me by engravings on stones . . . some lying askew, toppled by the silly acts of vandals. I felt a sense of peace, of serenity in this plot of earth. So far from my home, I felt at home.

As Peg and I drove away, still in a state of awe, I glanced casually at a structure standing almost obscured through the woods to our left. "My God, Peg, there it is! The old, brown photograph on the family wall. The family home. It's still there!"

We stopped the car and worked our way through the brush for a better view. A tall fence surrounds the property, but we found views for our cameras. Much grander than the old photograph portrayed. Three stories tall. White stone walls. A happy red tin roof. Six chimneys standing tall and proud. The first structure ever raised in the entire Greenville area. Completed in 1819 by my great-great-grandfather on land that he had purchased from the Cherokee Indians.

We learned the name of the occupants. A young couple with

two children. I called her. "Of course, we'd love for you to see the building. Please come in the morning."

As we approached the huge double front doors through which Grandmother Pryor had so often passed, I was overwhelmed with a sense of dèja vú. I could sense the anticipation of those who came to Captain Billy's house for the mail that was delivered only there for those who lived in a vast area of South Carolina. I could imagine the feeling of welcome experienced by the travelers whose stagecoaches stopped there to allow them to refresh themselves. Or perhaps to protect themselves, for some believe it was also used as a fort. I could see the young girl who became my grandmother running through that doorway with her rag doll. A stepping-stone to the front porch is a tombstone. The mason had carved out Captain William Young's last name on two lines. The "Youn" . . . on one line . . . then the "g" on the succeeding line. His wife Mary rejected the stone, and Captain Young became a stepping-stone for future generations. I know the feeling.

We explored the homeplace. Felt the coolness of stone walls over thirty inches thick. Felt the presence of kin, some of whom still visit in wisps of fog with echoed voices, according to our hostess. We climbed the stairway to the bedrooms. I knew it. I felt it before I saw it. There was where Carrie was born. That room was Grandmother's birthing room.

We climbed up to the attic . . . the original wooden beams still stand in firm support. No nails, wooden pegs still in place. We went down to the cellar and were haunted by the remnants of a tunnel that used to lead across the road. Why?

As we recorded our gracious hostess, I learned of other relatives. My great-great-great-grandfather was buried in nearby Spartenburg. A Baptist preacher. That's why I switched churches! And the first of the family, my great-great-great-great-grandfather. Buried in Jamestown . . . a member of the original colony after sailing the Atlantic from Wales.

Our new friend gave us ancient, crumbling letters found in the walls while restoration work was being done. As we scanned them, we read of Aunt Fanny and Aunt Alethea moving to Texas. (I remembered their biscuits and mustang grape jelly.) Precious words from the distant past now a part of us.

I left in a daze, but exhilarated, connected. I had come back to where I had never been. I had come back to the homeplace. Old times there are not forgotten.

THIRTY-FIVE

A Conversation with Michener

t was a perfect arrange-
ment. Author James Michener, who lives part of each year in
Austin, Texas, needed a photograph of himself with some Texas
authors. It was to be included in his forthcoming book, *The World
Is My Home*. I had long wished to interview Michener for my
radio show. A call from novelist Elizabeth Crook served the
purpose of both of us. She was inviting my wife and me for a
weekend with Michener, as well as authors Steve Harrigan and
Liz Carpenter, on her family's ranch up in the Texas Hill Country near Kerrville.

It was a weekend that called for out of doors. The tough
Texas summer had finally surrendered. The ranch house sits on
a high bluff overlooking a meandering river full of accommo-
dating bass, bream, and catfish. The curious sight of white-tailed
deer feeding with zebras or impalas below is not a rare one. A
neighbor raises exotic game that have little regard for segrega-
tion or fences. Elizabeth Crook's parents, Ambassador William

and Eleanor Crook (he's former ambassador to Australia) were relaxing hosts. Michener was in an expansive and comfortable mood following a Texas breakfast of huevos rancheros. I invited the other three writers to join me in the interview. We circled our chairs on the patio for the recording session.

I opened by asking Michener to use his gift for description and paint the scene we were viewing. He began, of course, with a typical Michener touch of historical reference.

"We are sitting on top of a cliff that Indians in past ages must have used as a lookout point, to watch what happens down in the valley and the river where animals are coming and to bag themselves a deer for dinner. We know that the Germans who were loyal to the Union in the Civil War, which most Germans in Texas were, came here on their way to escape. Right near here, they were booby-trapped by Southern loyalists and were eliminated, annihilated. We're on a cliff that allows us to see the wonderful way water, which is the lifeblood of Texas, comes through and waters this particular group of fields. Maybe five miles down there is a semidesert where there is no water. Believe me, when you are in a place like this, you are aware of water. And to see it must be very reassuring."

I asked him, as the world's greatest storyteller, how he became one.

"It started way back with me. I love to tell a story. I love to get things organized, to codify . . . love to put into hierarchy and am great at outlining, when I want to. I think that is all part of the storyteller's stock and trade. I also got to know great storytellers in the books I read. I remember the first boy's book I read was *Tom Swift and His Electric Rifle*. Tom got the electric rifle, and some baddies were trying to get the secret of it. Boy, did Tom take care of them! I thought that was quite wonderful . . . that the rifle itself was a major character in the story. It gave me an idea. It didn't have to be a man or woman. It could be a horse, eagle, or electric rifle. I think that love of storytelling is born in some people.

"You know, I never wrote anything until I was forty years

old. So I could have missed the whole ballgame. It was a very risky thing. I was one of the oldest men drafted in World War II. I was exempted from the draft. I was a Quaker. I could have pleaded religious exemption. I didn't. And I was older . . . could have claimed that, but I didn't. I saw Hitler and Tojo as world-class enemies, and I knew we would all be in it. When you are thirty-six and have that major disruption in the middle of your life, it's pretty shocking. I was out in the Pacific a long, long time. I had two tours in the Pacific. I knew an enormous number of men in World War II, my age, who when out in the Pacific decided, 'When I go back, I will not be the same jerk I was before.' Some of them went into politics. A surprising number of them went into religion. They wanted to count for something. So it was very common what I did . . . change. I wanted to be a writer."

Michener has a juicy sense of humor. Steve Harrigan wanted to explore it. "Mr. Michener, I notice in several of your books that the word 'scrapple' keeps coming up. Could you tell me what scrapple is?"

A mischievous glint in his eye as Michener took a deep breath in preparation of his response to this deeply probing question.

He said, "The world is divided in heaven because people from Pennsylvania Dutch country know what scrapple is . . . and revere it. And then there are you pathetic slobs from Arizona and Nevada who like grits. Someone said that when Carter went to the White House the northerners who wanted a job were in trouble when they went into a restaurant and ordered a grit."

We had a good laugh, but Steve, whom I suspect has scrappled, never got Michener's definition of scrapple.

Michener is a god to many. Few living authors are as revered. I wanted to know if this adulation ever got in his way as a writer.

"I receive an enormous amount of mail. Sometimes I have two or three secretaries helping me answer it because I do take it seriously. I try not to read the things that defame me because it tears me off my food, as they say. I don't read things that praise me highly. I don't think that's good for you. So I sort of go down the middle pretty much by myself and don't allow it to modify me one way or another. But I have to admit that if you sit in a little office in Austin, Texas, and get at least one letter a day . . . sometimes six or seven . . . saying your books have meant a great deal to somebody, it does count, and I prize that."

The Micheners are known for their generously spread philanthropy. They have given millions of dollars of art to the University of Texas. He has established fellowships for writers. This has been true wherever they have settled for awhile. Liz Carpenter wanted to know what prompted this generosity.

"My wife, Mari, and I were both recipients of free education from the United States. I went to nine colleges and universities, always at public expense. Never my own. Somebody else paid for the whole thing. My wife is of Japanese origin though born in the United States. She is a U.S. citizen. However, she was thrown into a concentration camp in the United States during World War II. She was taken out by a group of colleges that said, 'We can't waste these young people. They have to have an education.' So we both owe society an enormous debt. The only sensible thing to do is to repay it. But it isn't a big thing with us. What else would we do with our money?"

I was reluctant to ask this question because it's one that Barbara Walters would ask following a dramatic pause and with that pained expression on her face. But I wanted to know. "Jim, what do you fear?"

He was not insulted. He leaned back, crossed his arms, and placed his chin in one hand . . . that familiar thoughtful Michener pose . . . and said, "I have faced death far more often than most people. I have been at great revolutions. I have been at risk on patrols. I've been at risk . . . survived three airplane crashes where others have lost their lives. When that happens, you realize that you are home safe. This is a freebie. And if anything happens this afternoon, I'd have no complaints whatever. If a person lives to be sixty-three or sixty-four and is out of jail or the booby hatch, he's had a safe run. I have been removed from fear. I don't allow it."

I dared another Barbara Walterism: "What brings you joy?"

With Elizabeth Crook, James Michener, Liz Carpenter, and
Steve Harrigan. Photo by Peggy Davis Pryor.

"I love nature. I take a long walk every evening of my life. I
never tire of it . . . seeing trees, hearing the sounds . . . coming
to a wonderful place like this. It's a privilege I relish."

James Michener is probably our most entertaining historian. His books almost always deal with the past, and we learn so
much from his writing. But I wanted to know his perception of
our future as a nation.

"I have felt for a long time that the United States is safe to
about the year 2050. Now I first had that feeling at the year
1950, so I'm giving us about one hundred years. Obviously, a lot
of hundreds of years have been used up. But my crystal ball

doesn't go much longer than 2050 even today. I am constantly mindful of the overwhelming fact that all of the great civilizations I've written about have perished. The Greeks, the Romans, the Gallic one of Charlemagne, the British Empire, the great Spanish Empire, the Chinese Empire have perished. Now you and I have to be very arrogant or stupid to think that we are the only people who are exempt. We are not exempt. And what will be the path of our great decline, I am not wise enough to see. But I am scared as hell of some of the things I do see. Our shifting from a producing community to a consuming community. That's what Rome did and went down. I think our inability to settle the race problem is what did Greece in when they tried to have a society of slaves . . . the underprivileged. I think the most dangerous thing on the horizon for people like you and me is the decline of our schools . . . in the middle group. The top students are as good as they ever were. I see them all the time. Wonderful kids of Texas and Florida. The bottom group is the same in all societies at all times. Pretty hopeless. But the middle group who staff the nation and provide its strength and continuity is declining in value."

"And now, Jim, because of economic reasons, they are eliminating the arts from any schools." An immediate, passionate response.

"I think about that constantly." A moment of reflection, then, "Let us take a state like Ohio, where they idolize the Ohio State football team. Nothing finer than to be a halfback at Ohio State. The bulk of them never get a job in the big league. If they do, they don't stay in long enough even to get a pension. A very risky gamble they're on. And if Ohio State produced a Jack Nicholson, the great actor . . . or a Meryl Streep, an even greater actress . . . or an Emily Dickinson, who is going to write great poetry . . . or a Truman Capote, who writes those splendid stories, it would be so much more rewarding in the long haul. And I worry about that perversion of values. But it looks like we've launched into it, and there's nothing we can do about it. If we consistently denigrate the arts, music, sculpture, painting . . .

leave writing out of it . . . we cheapen our society, and we do it at our risk . . . we lessen our souls, absolutely. I don't apologize for art at all because I can see what it contributes to a society."

Elizabeth Crook, just beginning her promising career as a novelist, asked Michener to look back on his. "I was wondering if you have any regrets about your career . . . if you would have done anything differently."

He liked the question. And he said, "I have had a career that looks like an unbroken chain of successes, which in a way it has been. One big book after another. All top of the best-seller lists, and so on. But I've also had some real failures, things I started and was unable to finish. Real failures, costly of emotion and money spent. But nobody who has been divorced can claim life was an unqualified success because in that respect it sure as hell wasn't. I can go through quite a list of failures. I have been banned in many countries. I have been vilified. I have not had a clear sail at all. However, the failures seem so trivial in relation to the successes that I live with them. You bury them, and you don't become vengeful about it."

As I listened to the tape recording to recapture the words for this writing, I cringed at the next question I asked. But I'm glad I did. "Jim, you arrive at the Golden Gate. And St. Peter is introducing you to God, who doesn't read novels, but he wants to present you in the proper context. What should he say to her?" (That one was for Woman Activist Liz Carpenter.)

"I think I would like to be remembered as a man who was very willing to testify to his basic beliefs. I think if you read all my books there's a constant thread running through them of brotherhood . . . of fairness to other groups . . . of dignity for women . . . of the fact that a workman is worthy of a good wage. Those are the things that are very important to me. I am not a knee-jerk liberal. But when I see children dying in Africa, my knee jerks. When I see young black men in U.S. cities absolutely unable to get a job at all, my knee jerks. When I look at an S&L scandal in which we've been betrayed so badly, my knee jerks. And I hope it will always stay that way."

THIRTY-SIX

The Visitors

hey're like sunburn, heat rash, poison ivy, and bottoms become too large for the bikini. They come with the hot weather. The strange faces that suddenly appear at your office door and shout, "Hi! We're here."

And you fake it and say, "Well, by golly! So you are," wondering all the time who the heck they are.

It's the annual guessing-game time that coincides with summer vacations. Friends of long ago return, dragging their sunburned kids, and subject you to that horrible ritual of playing "Guess who?" Hell, I have to put name tags on my own kids. It isn't that you're not glad to see them. It's just often so difficult to know who you are being glad to see. So to help you in your annual identity dilemma, here are a few tips devised after too many years' experience that will enable you to avoid some of the embarrassment that comes with not remembering.

First of all, when you're greeted with, "Hi. We're here," respond, "Oh, my gosh. I was just thinking of you. Talk about a small world. As a matter of fact, I was telling one of my friends about you just the other day. I want him to meet you. Have a seat while I go and get him."

You then exit the room and find the guy that you've worked months to get the dirt on to make blackmailable. A good technique is to get a candid shot of him using the office copying machine for personal reasons. With the right lens, you can actually photograph that which he is copying. When it's time to work your blackmail, you simply show him the photographs and then say, "This is what I want you to do." He then gladly precedes your return to your office, greets your visitors with, "Hello. I'm a friend of your old buddy. He just got a call from the White House. Said to tell you he'd be right back. Well, he was telling me about you the other day. Boy, are you guys number one on his hit parade. Now, help me out. Who is who?"

They will naturally give him their names . . . and also, naturally, he will then depart the office, return to you, and tell you who they are. You then return in triumph, memory refreshed.

Another device that I find very effective is to keep a Polaroid camera in my desk at all times. As soon as I'm greeted with that "Hi, we're here" routine . . . and if I don't remember them from Eve, I say, "Well, sonofagun. Golly, don't you look great. Hey! Let me get a picture of you to show to the little lady." So you snap the picture. Of course, you've guessed the next part. You ask them to autograph their name right over their face. Then you can place the right name with the right face."

The old get well card works fine, too. It's a good summer saver. It's very simple. You keep a get well card stashed conveniently in your top desk drawer, next to the Polaroid. After the opening amenities, while you grope futilely for the names of your old friends, you say, "Hey, did you hear about old Sam?" Everyone knows a Sam. This puts them on the defensive in the name-guessing game. Turnabout is fair play. Then you say, "He was struck by a runaway pizza truck. Almost killed him. He's allergic to pepperoni. Hey, why don't you sign this get well card I'm sending him?" Naturally, they'd love to sign the get well card. And so they do . . . and then you get a little weller yourself by discovering their names. I usually give them a pencil with which to sign the card. Then I can later erase the names and use the card again on the next bunch.

Then there's the old mandatory IDs-for-security routine due to the number of threats recently received to blow up the building at any time. But that's another story.

Anyway, I hope this will help you survive those surprise visitors that will show up just as surely as fireants and freckles. Have a good summer.

THIRTY-SEVEN

Allison's Gift

ow do you tell her?
How do you tell a five-year-old girl, two weeks after her great-grandmother died, one week after her grandfather died . . . a week later, how do you tell her that her grandmother has just died, too? Sometimes Providence provides.

I am now my granddaughter Allison's only grandfather and my wife, Peggy, is her only grandmother. My daughter Kerry and her husband, Lee Roy Parnell, had made sure that their daughter Allison had prime time with her grandparents who lived in Stephenville, Texas. They had not had the privilege of knowing their grandfathers. They wanted their daughter to know hers. Lee Roy's father, Roy, was not in good health. They knew that his days on Earth were probably limited. They wanted Allison to experience Paw Paw's wonderful humor and storytelling. Roy became Allison's friend . . . as did her grandmother Anabelle and her great-grandmother Grandma Stone.

The great-grandmother's death did not come as a surprise.

She had been ill for some time. Allison accompanied her parents to Stephenville for the funeral. She did not attend the service, however. She was kept by a baby-sitter.

One week later came the sad news that Roy Parnell had passed away. Again the trip to Stephenville. Another funeral service. Another baby-sitter for Allison.

Seven days later, Lee Roy, a country music singer, received a telephone call following an engagement on the West Coast. An incredible shock. His mother, Anabelle, had died suddenly.

Kerry left Austin immediately to offer her help to Anabelle's stunned survivors in Stephenville. Lee Roy was flying in for yet another funeral.

Peggy and I kept Allison at our home in Austin until the day of the funeral. She was told only that her Nan Naw was sick and that Kerry was going to see her.

On the porch outside our bedroom, Peggy discovered the shell of a cicada, those noisy grasshopperlike critters that we hear all summer long in Texas. The shell was completely intact. Allison was fascinated by it. She had no fear of it and was very caring of it. "Where did he go when he left his shell, GrandPeggy?"

And Peggy replied, "He just came out and flew away. We don't know where he is, but we know he's okay. Like people when they die."

And Allison said, "Like my Paw Paw when he died."

Peggy placed the shell of the katydid in a small jewelry box on a bed of cotton. It looked like a tiny coffin.

When we drove Allison to Stephenville the next day, Peggy brought the insect along. Halfway there Allison asked where it was. "It's in a bag in the back of the car," said Peg. "I'll get it for you."

For the rest of the trip, Allison played with the shell which had a beautiful golden sheen to it, almost a glow. She played with it, and she thought about it.

She still did not know of her grandmother's death. However, we suspected she had concluded what had happened. As we neared the church where friends and relatives gathered for a luncheon preceding the funeral, Allison asked, "Will I have a babysitter after lunch like when Paw Paw died?"

When we arrived at the church, she was greeted by her father and mother. "Allison, darling, mother and daddy need to talk to you," her father said. They took her aside, she with her cicada clutched firmly in her little hands. She showed the shell of her new friend to them both.

"Allison, your Nan Naw has been very sick. And we've got something to tell you."

"Did she die?" asked the five-year-old.

"Yes," her father replied. "She was just like your little bug friend. She got tired of being in her body."

"Yes," said Allison excitedly. "She just flew out of there and went to heaven to be with God and Paw Paw and Grandma Stone. And we'll see them again sometime."

God gave Allison a cicada.

THIRTY-EIGHT

Saltwater Mustangs

or years they ruled the Texas Coast. The tarpon. Schools named their football teams after them. Inns bore their name. A sport-fishing industry was built around them. President Roosevelt came to Texas to fish for them. And then, they were gone. Not overnight, as vanished the sardines that made the economy of Monterey, California. But slowly, the tarpon that made the Texas Gulf Coast famous dwindled and dwindled in number. And finally, they were gone.

It was sad. Reasons were guesses—the factories built at the mouths of Texas rivers . . . the damming up of Texas tributaries . . . the netting of tarpon in Mexico to be sold as dog food. Perhaps, a combination of all these factors.

I used to fish only for these excitingly acrobatic silver kings. I've hooked scores and scores of the hard-mouth giants that can run over two hundred pounds. But I never landed one.

Then, recently came a call from my brother Bill in Houston, who retired as a flight controller for the FAA in order to fish more often. "I know a guide who fishes only for tarpon from June to October. He's at Galveston. I'm making a reservation for you and Dayne and me for August 25. Be there."

"But, Bill, there are no more tarpon in Texas."

"Be there!"

The guide's name is James Praag. He's one of those fishermen whose excitement for fishing is so intense he has no choice but to do it full time. His excitement is catching, even early in a coffeeless morning.

We didn't cruise from the marina at the Galveston Bay causeway to our destination, twenty or so miles away off the Bolivar Peninsula. We raced to it. We were about four miles offshore in a fairly calm sea. As we sped along in his twenty-four-foot open Boston Whaler, James' eyes were constantly scanning the water, doing what the seabirds were doing . . . looking for a sign, seeking fish. Endless miles of water and such a small area possibly occupied by the tarpon we were seeking. I felt more like a paleozoologist seeking an ancient fish than a guy trying to land a big one. I really believed the tarpon were gone from Texas.

Skeptically, I watched him bait the huge circular tuna hooks with shad and cast the lines out. There was another boat drifting about a half mile away. As I watched it, I saw a sight I hadn't seen in forty years. A leaping tarpon! Even that far away, I could see a flash of silver as the tarpon tried to throw the hook. My heart was leaping as high as the tarpon as I witnessed that incredible sight. A tarpon resembles a giant silver minnow with large scales. No fish is as acrobatic or as hard to land. It was a helluva show for about fifteen minutes. We watched them boat and release two silver kings. We also watched our rods bow to strikes, only to battle large sharks, not tarpon. Nine in all grabbed our baits.

We fished from 8:00 A.M. to 2:00 P.M. Disappointed, we prepared to return to the marina. But then came a radio call from a buddy guide. He had found them. "Come on over. It's alive with tarpon over here." We covered the two miles in seconds.

And there they were . . . cutting through the water like wild ocean mustangs. The area was alive with herds of tarpon, their huge silver sides flashing in the sunlight like mirrors. They were moving, porpoising, as they cruised the water with incredible speed.

James, now almost in a hysteria of excitement, stood on the bow, casting a lure into the middle of the schools as I steered the boat as we followed them. For over an hour, we chased the tarpon. We were Spanish *caballeros* in the middle of a stampede of mustangs . . . these water mustangs that have come back. Like J. Frank Dobie's mustangs in his book *The Mustangs* that had been vanishing, vanishing, vanished . . . now wild with sheer life . . . and free, free, free!

And they remained free. They would not take our bait. They were traveling, not feeding. But no matter. We had the visible truth that they are still here in Texas, like the salvaged brown pelicans and whooping cranes, and, hopefully, again multiplying in our Texas waters. The sight was worth the trip . . . the fatigue . . . even the long drive back home through Houston's forever going-home traffic.

THIRTY-NINE

Washington, D.C., Taxi

went to Washington, D.C., one day and got a fresh shot of patriotism. It came not in the halls of Congress nor from a speech by our president in the White House. It didn't come while standing at the foot of the Lincoln Memorial or while visiting the home of our first president, overlooking the Potomac. No, my Americanism rejuvenation came during a taxi ride to Washington's National Airport . . . through the fume-laden, traffic-clogged streets of our nation's capital.

Her name is Grace . . . another amazing Grace. Her taxi was her nest. As I entered, I encountered the pleasing smell of mint. The cab was clinically clean. Little doilies, apparently homemade, adorned the dashboard. On top of them were framed pictures of children and a soldier. Also, a wooden plaque that read: "God Bless America." Attached incredulously secure to the dashboard was an old-fashioned alarm clock. I would not have been surprised had she asked, "Would you like some fresh-baked cornbread?"

I was greeted with, "Good afternoon, sir. Are you leaving us today? Well, I know it will be good to get home. Where is your home? Texas, eh. I get lots of customers from Texas. I like Texans. They don't take themselves so serious as some of my customers do."

Within eight blocks, I had learned that Grace is a divorcée, mother of four. Two of her children are in college; another will attend. Her baby son is in the army. She remains good friends with her ex-husband, a barber, who still cuts her hair.

She asked me which airline I was flying. I told her American.

"That suits me just fine," she beamed. "If it's American it's gotta be great. This is the greatest country in the world. My son is in the army. That's him in the picture there on the sun visor. Isn't he a fine-looking boy? He's written me letters wherever he goes. He has given me a whole new appreciation of this country. No one has it as good as we Americans."

We were driving past the Washington Monument: "Now that's one man I would liked to have known. He was a soldier, too, you know. Not only led this country but fought to gain our freedom. He never did live in the White House. I took a passenger there yesterday. I wonder what Nancy is doing right now?"

I said, "Well, I suppose she and President Reagan are having their before-dinner cocktails."

"That's all right with me," she responded. "We can do whatever we're big enough to do in America."

Grace is the happiest taxi driver I've ever encountered. She kept up a steady stream of chatter even as she expertly wove her way through the afternoon going-home rush hour traffic.

"How do you account for your happiness?" I asked.

"Because I live in America. I had a wonderful father and mother. I went to fine schools here in Washington. Being a black didn't get in the way of me learning things. I've got four wonderful children, and they're all getting along fine in life. I know that we've got lots of problems, especially in this town. But you know, we've got a lot of wonderful people trying to figure out how to solve them because they care. And as long as we care and keep on trying, we're gonna be just fine. Why shouldn't I be happy? I say God bless America."

As she deposited me at Washington National, she thanked me for my business, and I thanked her for a crash course in America appreciation . . . delivered in the least likely school in the world . . . a Washington, D.C., taxi.

Flying back home that evening, I reflected on Grace and the larger than usual tip I left her. Did I buy into yet another flag-waving for profit routine? I think not. But if I did, it was worth the ride.

FORTY

The Loser

She drove up to the convenience store in an automobile that yelled, "Help!" It appeared to be not on its last mile but its last block. The woman, too, seemed to be far beyond her warranty. Many miles she had seen.

She rushed into the store with a sense of urgency that bordered on emergency. In a few moments, she returned to her car. Frantically she went through what appeared to be about twenty-dollars worth of lottery cards. After scratching the stars off a card, she would throw it into the backseat to mingle with the remnants of a life built of throwaways. This done, she rushed back into the store. She returned with another handful of lottery coupons. Again she repeated the same process of disgustedly tossing the wrong numbers onto the backseat. A third time . . . and the third time, she failed again. Now the face was defeated. It had not the strength to display anger or disappointment. It could only droop . . . give way to gravity . . . to pain . . . to despair.

She turned the key to the ignition of her gravely ill car . . . it whined twice with the effort . . . and then weakly hummed that dreaded tune of no more to give. A man in an adjacent battered pickup, also examining lottery tickets, saw the woman's dilemma. Without a word, he got his often-used jump start cables from his toolbox, opened the hood of her car, attached the cables . . . and then spoke, "Give her a try." She did . . . and it did. He retrieved his cables, gave her a little wave, and she chugged away, probably wondering if she had enough gas to get home . . . if she had one. Maybe she was riding in it.

That evening one of my granddaughters was given two lottery cards. She didn't even know the meaning of the word gambling. The first card she processed, with instructions, awarded her two dollars. "Gee, this is fun!"

You could see the wheels spinning in her brain . . . roulette-like. Later that evening, we went out for supper. The same granddaughter spotted a glass cage full of teddy bears, dogs, cats . . . furry things. For a quarter, you had the opportunity to operate the mechanical tongs that you hoped would lift one of the stuffed animals into your possession. Chances poor to slim. However, on her first attempt, the little girl lifted a teddy bear out of its prison. "Hey, this is easy! Let's try some more."

There were enough uncles and grandparents there to finance several more tries. But the machine had lost its generosity and had been paid several times for the teddy bear it had surrendered.

I was thinking, "I wonder if this granddaughter has inherited the genes of her mother's father, who lost the family ranch several times in card games? And then lost it forever . . . as well as his family?" Time will tell. Government will provide her a lifetime of opportunities to test her genetic gambling tendencies. But government is benevolent. It has provided a free 1-800 number for those with compulsive gambling tendencies.

FORTY-ONE

The Hands of Time

was standing where the land ends and the ocean begins, watching my grandchildren play in that transitional zone. They were at the shallow age. The breaking waves and deeper water will come later. They were filling their buckets with sand and filling their souls with the sea. It was a beautiful sight.

Tiny arms and legs like Tootsie Rolls . . . brown but with white bands where the sun didn't penetrate the crevices. Sunbonnets protecting the vulnerable faces. They looked like very small pioneer women.

As I observed them, I became conscious of what I was doing with my hands. I was clasping my hands behind my back. And I thought, I have reached the hands-behind-the-back age. My God! Does that make me a sage? I have always been conscious of those men who assume that stance. Newsreels of ancient statesmen in places like Geneva, London, Paris, strolling in lovely gardens or halls of state discussing weighty matters of the world, their hands clasped behind their backs.

I remember old films of Einstein almost always with his hands clasped behind his back. Sir George Bernard Shaw was a hands-behind-the-back clasper. Surely Abraham Lincoln was one, too. And certainly George Washington often so stood on his front porch overlooking the Potomac, considering the future of this new country.

It is a noble stance. It says things. When your hands are behind your back, you are choosing to be vulnerable. The vulnerability of the venerable. For with your hands behind you, you are open to attack. And you are saying, "I am without fear. I am at peace. I am wise with age. I have warded off a lifetime of invasions with my hands. When I was but a boy, I learned to have my hands ready to ward off blows from my big brother or my playmates. And then I learned to use them offensively."

As I grew older, I learned that it wasn't easy to know what to do with my hands when talking to a girl. And then I remembered why they made pockets. And that's where I put my hands. Later I learned how much trouble you can get into with your hands and girls.

In elementary school, I noted that "sissies" used their hands like girls do. I learned that "regular fellers" are supposed to disdain boys who use their hands like girls. Like carrying your books held up to your chest. Later I discovered that those male hands could write beautiful poems and music and stories and build beautiful buildings and communities and heal and do all kinds of wonderful things.

Then I discovered that you could send messages by where you placed your hands. Standing erect with your legs spread wide and your hands made into fists placed on your hips meant "I am tough." Likewise, standing with your thumbs hooked into your belt. "Resolute. Immovable. Don't tread on me." Two hands placed behind the head meant, "I'm comfortable with you . . . with life." Place your left hand under your right armpit and place the right hand under your chin and extend your right forefinger to the cheek and you appear thoughtful. Place the entire right hand as a fist under the chin and you're in deeper thought. *The Thinker.*

As I grew into manhood, I learned that how you handled your hands could send various messages of sophistication. Arms folded in front of you can mean a closed mind, a resoluteness if you bury your hands into your armpits. But if you fold your arms and grasp the upper part of the arm with your hands you convey a man thinking. Or listening. It is also a common gesture of being uncomfortably cold and a subtle hint to whomever is in charge of the thermostat to turn it up.

I've always admired Italian hands. They are so expressive, so dramatic, so natural. Italian hands are part of their language.

I remember my hands-in-my-hip-pockets stage. This positioning denotes a good listener. Also, a comfortable listener. It's a good position for observing beauty . . . a landscape, real or painted. Hearing a beautiful song. Making pictures out of clouds. Watching a baby asleep. And the hands in the hip pocket could possibly be an evolutionary stage . . . perhaps the last step before reaching where I discovered on the beach I now am. A hands-clasped behinder.

There is a traditional final hands position. Arms crossed over the chest with each hand grasping the opposite upper arm. The signal of curtains. Not for me. I want to check out of this world with my arms behind my back. So they will say, "My, how wise he looks."

On Mustang Island. Photo by Peggy Davis Pryor.

Index

A

Aaker, Linda, 79, 80, 81, 82
Adair, Red, 116
Adenauer, Chancellor, 120, 122
Alaska, 17, 18, 19, 20, 21
Ali, Muhammad, 44
Alice, Texas, 4
Amarillo, Texas, 54, 55, 56, 57, 58, 59
Arkansas, 11
Armstrong, Bob, 79, 80
Armstrong, Shannon, 79
Arness, James, 115
Austin, Texas, 2, 5, 11, 38, 40, 46, 54, 56, 67, 82, 86, 95, 108, 109, 114, 115, 120, 129, 132
Axum, Donna, 27, 28, 29 (photo)

B

Ball, Lucille, 14, 115
Blocker, Dan, 115
Bolton, Paul, 5, 30
Boone, Jean, 29
Brill, Idanell, 95
Brooks, Foster, 44
Brown, John Y., 44
Bulloch, Joshua, 47, 48, 49, 50
Bush, George, 114

C

Campbell, Earl, 68
Carpenter, Liz, 2, 17, 129, 132, 133 (photo), 135
Carter, Jimmy, 114, 131
Channing, Carol, 115
Christoffersen, Ana Christina, 11

Christoffersen, Thomas, 11
Clark, Julie, 26
Clark, Stuart, 26
Cohen, Ethyl, 73
Cohen, Julie, 72
Connally, Idanell "Nellie" Brill, 95, 96 (photo)
Connally, John, 95, 96 (photo), 97, 98, 99
Corpus Christi, Texas, 51
Crawford, Joan, 115
Crenshaw, Ben, 53
Cronkite, Walter, 14
Crook, Eleanor, 130
Crook, Elizabeth, 129, 134
Crook, William, 129

D
Dailey, Dan, 7
Davis, James, 120, 121, 122, 123
Dempsey, Mike, 2
Dornoch, Scotland, 80
Dounie, Scotland, 80, 81

E
Erhard, Ludwig, chancellor of West Germany, 120

F
Father Damien, 105, 106
Faulk, John Henry, 40, 42 (photo), 44, 73, 124
Fonda, Jane, 5, 6
Ford, Gerald, 114
Ft. Benning, Georgia, 116
Furnam University, 125

G
Galveston Bay, Texas, 143

George, Phyllis, 43, 44, 45 (photo), 46
Godfrey, Arthur, 5
Greenville, South Carolina, 11, 124, 125, 126

H
Hana, Hawaii, 33
Harrigan, Steve, 129, 131, 133 (photo)
Hayes, Helen, 29 (photo), 115
Headliners Club, The, 14, 15
Heatherton, Joey, 67, 68
Heloise, 17
Herzog, Leo, 111
Heston, Charleton, 115
Hobltizell, Karl, 67
Hodgson, Jay, 28, 29
Holberg, Mike, 4
Hope, Bob, 66, 67, 68, 69, 115
Humphrey, Hubert, 120
Hunter, Alexander, 78, 79, 80, 81
Hunter, David, 78, 79, 80, 81 (photo)
Hunter, Jeremy, 78, 79, 80, 82
Hunter, Julia, 78, 79, 80, 81 (photo)

J
Jackson, Carolyn, 27
Johnson, Lady Bird, 7, 38, 46, 95, 114, 120, 121, 122, 123
Johnson, Lyndon Baines, 38, 96, 98, 114, 116, 117, 118, 121, 122

K
Kahn, Ayub, 120
Kamehameha V, King, 101, 105

Kauai, Hawaii, 60, 61
KBKI, 7
Kennedy, John F., 5, 98, 120, 122
King Ranch, 18
Kite, Tom, 89
KLBJ, 2, 7, 38
KNOW, 7
KNUZ, 5, 7
KSIX, 7
KTBC, 7, 95, 96
KTBC-TV, 7
Kuralt, Charles, 2, 5

L
LBJ Ranch, 5, 120, 121, 122
Lindbergh, Charles, 33, 34, 35, 36
Longhorn Club, The, 14
Los Angeles, California, 22, 23, 24
Love, Dan, 28, 29
Lufkin, Texas, 63
Lundquist, Vern, 30

M
Majors, Lee, 44
Mann, Rev. Dr. Gerald, 6, 87, 88 (photo), 89
Marks, Richard, 102, 103, 105, 106
Marsh III, Stanley, 54, 55, 56, 57 (photo), 58, 59
Martin, Dean, 115
Maui, Hawaii, 33, 35, 36, 38, 39, 100
McMurray, Fred, 115
Michener, James, 129, 130, 131, 132, 133 (photo), 134, 135
Michener, Mari, 132

Miller, Barbara, 17, 28
Molokai, Hawaii, 100, 101, 102, 105, 106, 107
Mother Theresa, 107
Mount McKinley, Alaska, 57
Moyers, Bill, 30, 46
Mt. Bonnell, 40
Mustang Island, Texas, 1, 51, 90

N
Normandy, France, 92, 93, 94

O
O'Donnell, Bob, 67
Ozarks (Arkansas), 17

P
Parnell, Allison, 26, 139, 140, 141
Parnell, Anabelle, 139, 140
Parnell, Lee Roy, 139, 140
Peaceful Mountain, Alaska, 20
Peck, Gregory, 14, 115
Pedernales River, 5
Peppard, George, 115
Pickle, Gary, 89
Pickle, Jake, 96
Port Aransas, Texas, 75, 91
Praag, James, 143
Presley, Elvis, 27
Pryor, Ana Louise 26
Pryor, Bill, 142
Pryor, Caroline Wallace, 11, 65, 125, 127
Pryor, Dayne, 3, 72, 78, 79, 80
Pryor, Don, 3, 26
Pryor, Elizabeth Jewell, 26, 73, 74
Pryor, John, 12
Pryor, Julie Cohen, 26, 72

Pryor, Kerry, 3, 26, 73, 139, 140
Pryor, Marissa, 26, 74
Pryor, Mary, 73
Pryor, Paul, 3, 26, 74
Pryor, Pecos, 26, 74
Pryor, Peggy, 2, 11, 12, 55, 60,
    61, 70, 73, 80, 81 (photo), 91,
    100, 101, 102, 125, 126, 139,
    140
Pryor, Richard "Skinny," 12,
    108, 109, 110 (photo), 111
Pryor, Sam, 37, 38
Pryor, Wallace, 12
Pryor, Wallace "Wally," 27, 30

R
Radio stations: KBKI, 7; KLBJ,
    2, 7, 38; KNOW, 7; KNUZ,
    5, 7; KSIX, 7; KTBC, 7, 95,
    96
Reagan, Ronald, 114, 146
Redfield, Arkansas, 49
Rio Grande Valley, Texas, 4, 23
Riverbend Baptist Church, 89
River Carron, Scotland, 80
Royal, Coach Darrell, 13, 14, 15
    (photo), 16, 115

S
San Antonio, Texas, 85
Sawyer, Kim, 81
Segal, Rabbi Jack, 73, 74
Silver Creek, Alaska, 19, 20
Smertz, Mr. and Mrs. Leonard,
    112

Stephenville, Texas, 139, 140
Stewart, James, 115
Stone, Grandma, 139, 141

T
Television stations: KTBC-TV,
    7
Thomas, Danny, 115
Thompsen, Marinus, 11

U
UCLA, 22, 66
University of Texas, 5, 95, 132

W
Wahl, Willy, 2
Wallace, Jack, 29
Walters, Barbara, 132
Wayne, John, 114, 115, 116, 117
    (photo), 118, 119
Wayne, Patrick, 117
Welch, Raquel, 115
Williams, Andy, 44
Williams, Jaston, 14
Willie, Raymond, 118

Y
Yates, Walter, 17, 18 (photo), 19,
    20, 21
Young, Captain William, 125,
    127
Young, Mary, 125, 127

Z
Zoppi, Tony, 67, 68

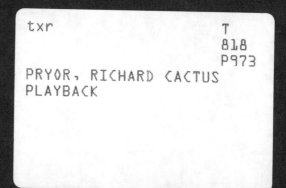